Hellertown, Pa.

Colonial Home Plans

Colonial Home Plans

Selected by the editors of
Hudson Home Guides

BANTAM/HUDSON PLAN BOOKS

New York, New York • Los Altos, California

COLONIAL HOME PLANS

A Bantam Book/published in association with
Hudson Home Publications
First Printing, April 1977
Second Printing, February 1978

Executive Editor, Robert J. Dunn; Book Editor, Sandra L.
Beggs; Project Editor, Bill Rooney; Art Director, Carolyn
M. Thompson; Cover Design & Rendering, Kenneth Vendley;
Book Design, Annette T. Yatovitz; Graphics, Dean C. Holmer;
Plans Service, Elayne Pappis, Charlene Azucena, Sandy Rollings.

Cover plan appears on page 12.

ISBN 0-553-01075-1

Published simultaneously in the United States and Canada

Bantam Books are published by Bantam Books, Inc. Its trade-
mark, consisting of the words "Bantam Books" and the portrayal
of a bantam, is registered in the United States Patent Office and
in other countries. Marca Registrada. Bantam Books, Inc. 666
Fifth Avenue, New York, New York 10019.

Printed in the United States of America.
Library of Congress catalog card number 76-52847.

ABOUT THIS BOOK . . .

Whether your new home dream is an immediate one or off on the horizons of your future, this book can be a tremendous aid in the planning process if you're thinking of building an Early American home. The architectural styles of these 70 pre-designed plans include the complete range of design variations inherent in the evolution of our American home building heritage. You can purchase a set to study in detail. Analyze how the floor plan fits your special needs or, perhaps with some professional assistance, ascertain what modifications you can make to the basic plan in order to make it precisely the home you have dreamed about. Review other plans carefully. Often you will find elements you like, for example, in a floor plan that could be designed into an overall plan or elevation that suits you otherwise. Many of the plan packages have materials lists, some don't. Many quality builders prefer to specify their own materials because of their familiarity with what is readily available in their building areas as well as relative price structures that vary considerably across the country. If you're ready to build, and are convinced you've found just the right plan for you, we'd strongly suggest that you purchase a minimum of four, if not six or eight sets for the use and convenience of your lender, contractor, subcontractor and others involved in the soul-satisfying process of bringing your new home dream to a reality.

The Pre-designed Plan

Any style of home — Modern, Victorian, Contemporary, Georgian or Colonial — starts with a concept on paper that is modified, revised and improved until it evolves into a workable and attractive plan. It may take a talented architect months or even years to develop a unique custom home design. Not everyone can afford the time or cost of a private architect, and unless you are faced with an exceptionally difficult building site or desire a one-of-a-kind home, the architect may not be necessary. In fact, today, approximately 80 percent of single-family and vacation homes are built without the direct involvement of an architect.

At the other end of the cost/time scale, some families choose a pre-manufactured home built from a stock plan in panelized or modular sections on a factory assembly line, which can be erected in a matter of a few short weeks. This pre-packaged home approach can be quick, relatively free of code and material problems and can represent a sound value. Yet many people find the available models too limiting in design, choice of materials and floor plan flexibility to meet their needs.

Between the custom architect and the pre-packaged building concept, lies the method chosen by many families to achieve their dream home — the pre-designed plan. This decision is not just a compromise, rather it is an opportunity to gain the best features of the alternate methods and overcome many of their shortcomings at the same time.

PRE-DESIGNED HOMES

Producers of pre-designed home plans offer a selection of sizes and styles to match almost every conceivable set of family needs, tastes and budget restrictions. Throughout the following pages of this book, you will discover Colonial plans ranging from snug Cape Cod designs to sprawling five and six bedroom Early American farm homes.

Who creates these plans? They are developed by either individual architects, designers or by commercial plan services. The plans developed by these professionals are historically accurate and yet take full advantage of the latest construction techniques and newest building materials. These licensed architects and designers meet all the requirements necessary to assure well-designed, safe and highly functional plans.

Their creative layouts can be purchased directly from the various plan services, from the individual architect or through magazines and books such as this which offer pre-designed plans for sale. Depending upon the designer and the size and complexity of the home, single plan sets usually range from $50 to $100.

WHAT'S IN THE PLAN PACKAGE?

You receive a complete set of working drawings as detailed as you'd obtain from a custom architect. The plans are detailed enough to satisfy local building officials when securing various building permits or requesting zoning variances. Plan sets are used with lending agencies when arranging financing for a construction loan, material suppliers when figuring the cost of lumber, plywood and roofing and, from the plans, a builder can estimate his labor costs. And finally, they can be used during actual construction of the home.

Although the plan package may differ slightly from supplier to supplier, most plan sets include a basement and foundation plan, detailed floor plans for each level, four-sided exterior elevation drawings and interior elevation details of special features such as kitchen cabinet work, fireplaces and cutaway sections and drawings of framing and construction details. The basic plan set usually includes a materials list spelling out the quality of various components, i.e. specie and grade of lumber, thickness and type of plywood, size and weight of shingles, etc. Some, but not all plans, list the actual quantity of materials and often specify by brand name. However, since changes are often made prior to or during construction, the quantity materials list may be offered for a nominal additional charge by plan services. Some plan packages may include electrical or wiring diagrams but, since requirements may vary across the country, specific plumbing, heating and cooling information may be omitted.

Occasionally you may find a home plan that looks

like the perfect answer to your family's needs but the orientation is wrong for your particular site. Many plan companies solve this problem by offering a mirror or full reverse floor plan at no additional cost if specified or for a modest extra charge. Since pre-designed plans are created to adapt to most average building sites and meet the demands of normal family living, they may not always fit your particular needs. Plan designers recognize this fact and expect that a few minor changes in specifications may be necessary. In fact, they often encourage these changes by offering alternate interior design options. For instance, the basic plan may call for three bedrooms and a separate dining room, while an optional plan, in the same amount of space, offers four bedrooms and a combination kitchen-family room layout.

SELECTING THE "RIGHT" PLAN
A Colonial home of your own. You've been thinking about it for months, perhaps years, and now is the time to search for that perfect plan. Your new home must be cozy and inviting, something you'll be proud to live in with your family and enjoy with your friends. It should project the warmth and charm of honest Colonial styling yet be efficient and livable at the same time. The floor plan should allow for those quiet moments in your life and at the same time be equipped to handle active family living. And it must have a fireplace or two and a compact kitchen that's both traditional and up-to-the-minute. And don't forget storage space, lot's of it, and maybe a sewing room and a workshop off the garage. Then it's got to be large enough for privacy and small enough to be easily maintained and . . . well, it must be a lot of different things to many people. And finally, your dream must somehow fit within your budget. It all sounds like an impossible challenge for one single plan.

However, before you begin the search for that perfect pre-designed home plan, there are several important considerations to be explored. One of the most basic is a thorough understanding of what you and your family expect from your new home. How much living and storage space is necessary? What are

your patterns of eating and entertaining? Recreation? Hobbies? Number of children, ages and their special demands? Are you a quiet family group or a fun loving mob with a constant stream of friends and visitors descending on your home? All of these questions and the many more they suggest should be talked over with the family before you can hope to fully understand the type of home plan you are seeking. Invest the time to explore these answers thoroughly before launching your plan search.

Have you chosen the building lot yet? It is often impossible to make a final plan selection without having a definite site in mind. Get to know your property, weigh the possibilities and learn the restrictions. Is the land level or steeply sloped? What are the soil conditions and drainage? Where should the driveway be located? Which direction should the house face? What are the wind, sun and shade patterns at different times of the day? Where is the best view and what are the landscaping possibilities? What is the approximate price range and style of surrounding homes? All these questions have a direct bearing on the home plan you finally select.

Other considerations include zoning regulations which often affect the type of house, number of stories, the maximum and minimum square footage either permitted or required for a lot your size along with set-back and fence height restrictions for the area. Local building codes may demand certain types and grades of materials, number of doors, types and sizes of windows and electrical, heating and sanitary regulations which must be met.

Before making your plan selection, one final subject must be explored. Cost! There is absolutely no way around it. Building and maintaining a home costs money. At times you will need cash and at other times, a long term loan or credit to finance the actual construction. You have to shop for money just as you would any other item. And it pays to check around to find the best terms. Just saving a fraction of a percentage point adds up quickly when spread over the life of a long term loan.

continued

When totaling your money needs, be sure to include all items. Land and closing costs, design and plan fees, labor and materials. Then add in interest costs, taxes and insurance. Now figure the cost of furnishing your new home and estimate the operating expense of monthly utility, telephone and maintenance charges. Most experts figure two percent of the cost of an average home should be set aside annually to cover normal maintenance.

How do you figure the various costs on a home whose plan you haven't even selected yet? With a little research, you can come up with some realistic guidelines. A local real estate agent or your city building department can supply average land and building costs for the area. For instance, their records may indicate that most homes are constructed in the $25 to $26 per square foot range, exclusive of land costs. This means that a 2,000 square foot home will cost in the neighborhood of $40-42,000. Your banker can help with information on interest, taxes and insurance costs and the local utility, because of their knowledge of energy rates and local temperature extremes, and can supply reasonable heating and cooling cost estimates. The aim of this cost research is to determine the approximate monthly dollar figure you can comfortably afford during construction and while living in your newly built home.

The quickest way to launch the actual plan search is to review the various pre-designed plans offered in magazines and books. Here, you won't find the detailed information offered in the actual plan set, but the publications will illustrate "presentation plans" which usually include a front exterior elevation sketch of the home with simplified floor plans drawn to scale. At a glance, you can evaluate the general appearance of the home and determine the number of bedrooms,

baths and the traffic flow patterns of the activity areas. The total square footage figure will provide an approximate construction cost.

You may find several presentation plans that look promising. At this stage, it can be worth your while to purchase a complete set of several plans for careful scrutiny. The modest investment now is good insurance against expensive mistakes later. Seriously examine the complete sets of working drawings to determine the merits of each home plan. Which direction should the doors open to avoid confusion in the halls? Should the patio door slide left or right? What optional floor plans does the designer suggest?

CUSTOMIZING YOUR PLANS
One of the advantages of pre-designed plans is that they permit a degree of flexibility. If your plan does not offer the options you need, perhaps your builder can suggest changes and redraw the plans. A better solution, particularly where a difficult building site or building codes require technical modifications, is to hire a local architect on an hourly consulting basis ($20 to $40 per hour) and work out the necessary changes. Major design or structural changes, moving walls, relocating plumbing, etc., should be avoided. Also, remember that you cannot interchange features from one plan to another without destroying the integrity of the original design. Material substitutions, however, are easily accommodated.

After the plan has been chosen or modified, you will need four to eight complete sets for use with lending agencies, local building departments, estimators, builders and subcontractors. Selecting the right plan and completing your home is well worth the effort. Somewhere out there, your pre-designed Colonial dream home plan is waiting.

How Important are Specifications?

Specifications are an essential part of the total plan. You and your architect must specify as thoroughly and accurately as possible exactly how your home is to be constructed and what materials and finishes are to be used. The specifications represent a contract or agreement between you and the builder as to what will be supplied and how it will be installed. Remember that your contractor can be held legally responsible for only the materials described and if items are vague, instructions incomplete or omitted, you'll probably end up paying extra. Check all specifications carefully before the job is begun and avoid making changes during construction.

14. **LATH AND PLASTER:**
Lath ☐ walls, ☐ ceilings: Material .... ; weight or thickness
Dry-wall ☑ walls, ☑ ceilings: Material ....*sheet rock*....... ; thickness...*½*...
.......*Tape and finish as recommended by the manufactu*

15. **DECORATING:** (Paint, wallpaper, etc.)

ROOMS	WALL FINISH MATERIAL AND APPLICATION
Kitchen	*Pinehill paneling, Georgia Pacific*
Bath	*2 coats flat oil*
Family Room	*Rio Grande paneling, georgia Pacy*
all other	*sheet rock and 2 coats latex*

16. **INTERIOR DOORS AND TRIM:**
Doors: Type ...*Pine panel*... ; material
Door trim: Type ...*moulded*... ; material ...*Pine*... Base:
Finish: Doors ...*stain, 2 coats clear finish*... ; trim
Other trim (item, type and location) ...*all trim will have 2 0 - —*

How to Read Building Blueprints

Every home plan details hundreds of building components, appliances and fixtures. To spell out each item would fill the page so architects have developed a set of standard symbols to represent most of the common elements. In order to understand blueprints, you have to be able to view a two-dimensional drawing and imagine or visualize a three-dimensional space. Learn to mentally walk through the home. By knowing a few basic symbols, you gain a much better understanding of how the home was designed to function.

In the kitchen, for instance, you can see the relationship between the sink, range and refrigerator, estimate the amount of cabinet space and imagine the number of steps necessary to serve dinner or get breakfast on the table. Doors indicate the direction of swing and a different symbol is used for sliding closet or patio doors. This helps you plan furniture arrangements. The shorthand symbols are the same on all pre-designed plan sets. Those shown below represent some you're likely to see most often.

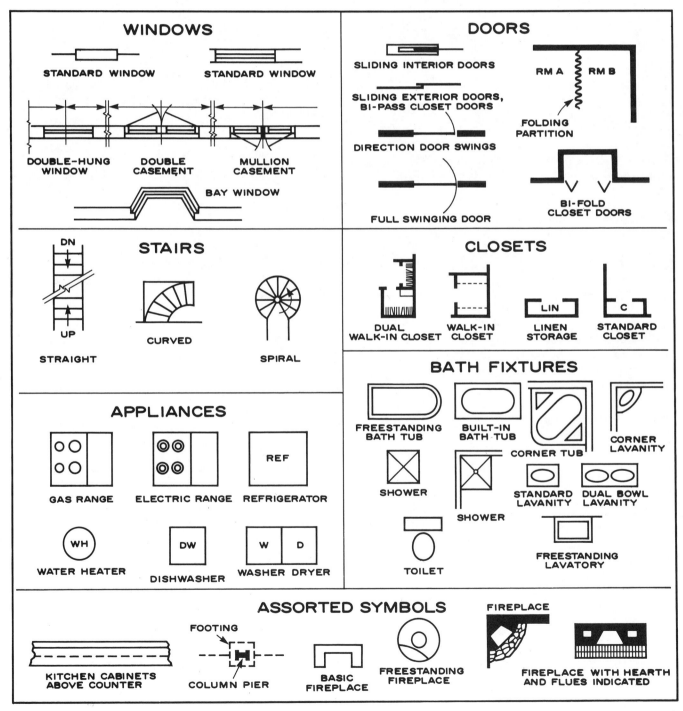

Colonial living centers around three fireplaces

PLAN 5904

A classic two-story Colonial plan, based on a home first built in 1753 in Fairfield, Connecticut, revolves around three large fireplaces. An alternate second floor plan allows a four or five bedroom home. The efficient U-shaped kitchen with adjacent family room, first floor lavatory and two full baths on the second floor handle the requirements of a large family. Generous closet space on both floors and a double car garage add to the livability. Mirror reverse plans available if specified at no additional cost; materials list included.

Designer: Evan Pollitt, Architect

First Floor . . . 1594 sq. ft.
Second Floor . . . 1325 sq. ft.
Basement . . . 1594 sq. ft.

Early American styling inside and out

PLAN 2033

From the exterior, this 1½-story home features the "added-on" look typical of early Colonial construction. Narrow siding and corner boards, copper roof over the bay window plus shutters and garage cupola complete the traditional feeling. The beamed cathedral ceiling and oversized fireplace in the sunken living room back up the built-in barbecue unit in the family room. Mirror reverse plans for the five bedroom, three full bath home are available if specified at no additional cost. Materials list is included.

Designer: Master Plan Service

Second Floor . . . 477 sq. ft.

First Floor . . . 1782 sq. ft.

TO ORDER
BUILDING BLUEPRINTS
USE ORDER FORM
ON PAGE 111

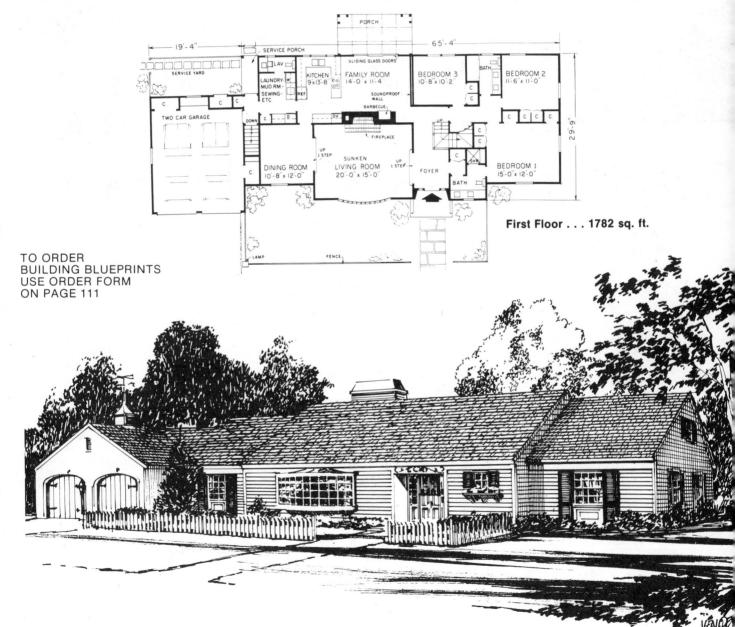

Design bespeaks the personal touch

PLAN 4204 (3-bedroom plan)
PLAN 4204-A (4-bedroom plan –
please specify)

This comfortable, traditional home plan offers several options for personal expression in exterior treatment, while still preserving the architectural design. A fourth bedroom can be added over the family room. Appearance of the facade can be varied with an overhang and choice of styles in doorways, walkway and garage. Mirror reverse plans are available if specified.

Designer: Claude Miquelle Associates

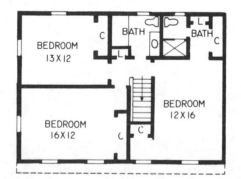

Second Floor:
4-Bedroom Plan . . . 1080 sq. ft.
3-Bedroom Plan . . . 816 sq. ft.

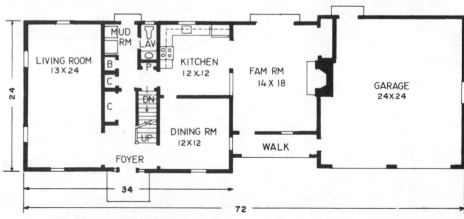

First Floor . . . 1080 sq. ft.

Traditional aura...modern living

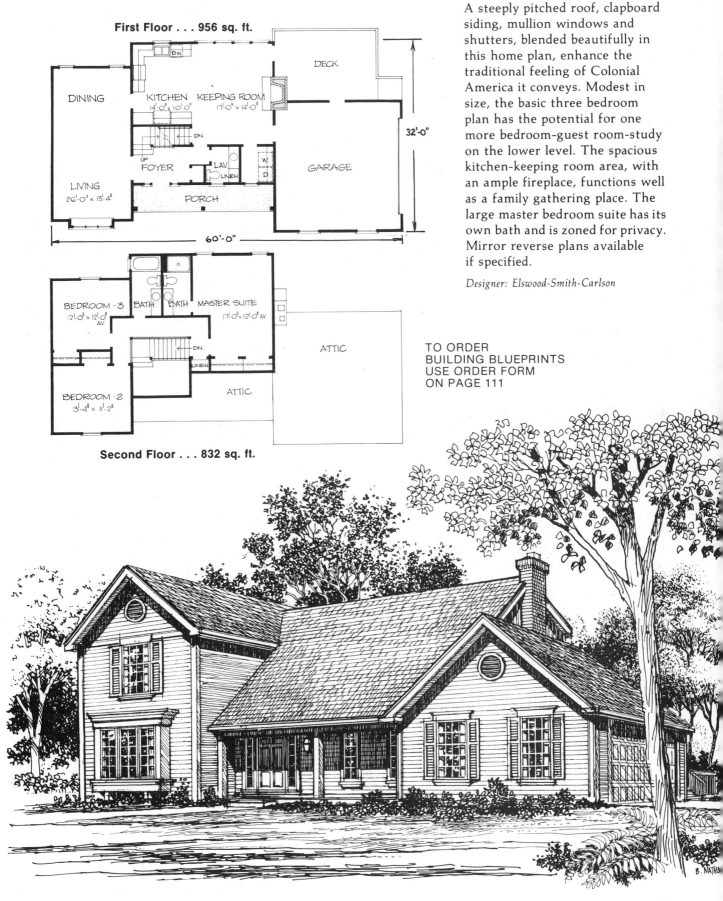

First Floor . . . 956 sq. ft.

DINING

KITCHEN
14'-0" x 10'-0"

KEEPING ROOM
17'-0" x 14'-0"

D.W.

DECK

32'-0"

DN.

UP

FOYER

LAV.

LINEN

W.
D.

GARAGE

LIVING
26'-0" x 13'-4"

PORCH

60'-0"

BEDROOM-3
12'-0" x 12'-0"
AV.

BATH

BATH

MASTER SUITE
17'-0" x 12'-0" AV.

ATTIC

DN.

LINEN

BEDROOM-2
13'-4" x 11'-2"

ATTIC

Second Floor . . . 832 sq. ft.

PLAN 3411

A steeply pitched roof, clapboard siding, mullion windows and shutters, blended beautifully in this home plan, enhance the traditional feeling of Colonial America it conveys. Modest in size, the basic three bedroom plan has the potential for one more bedroom-guest room-study on the lower level. The spacious kitchen-keeping room area, with an ample fireplace, functions well as a family gathering place. The large master bedroom suite has its own bath and is zoned for privacy. Mirror reverse plans available if specified.

Designer: Elswood-Smith-Carlson

TO ORDER
BUILDING BLUEPRINTS
USE ORDER FORM
ON PAGE 111

B. NATHAN

Early American farmhouse styling

PLAN 2322

The natural finish of weathered shingles on the exterior reflect the simple honest styling of this two-story Colonial, based on the home where Walt Whitman was born. The covered porch directly off the living room can be converted into a future family room. The living room fireplace features a log storage cabinet accessible from the porch. Separate dining room, kitchen with generous cabinet space, compact dinette and mud-laundry room overlook the large rear patio. Foyer hall has a lavatory hidden behind the main stair. The second floor has three bedrooms and two baths, one directly off the master bedroom. Plans include full basement information and material list. Mirror reverse plans are available for $10 extra.

Designer: Samuel Paul, AIA

TO ORDER
BUILDING BLUEPRINTS
USE ORDER FORM
ON PAGE 111

Second Floor . . . 720 sq. ft.

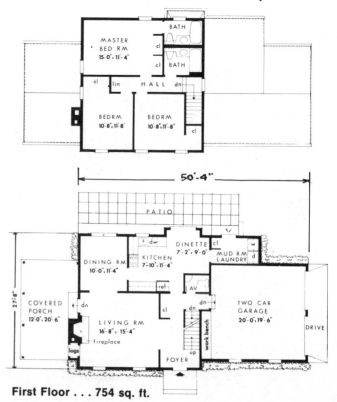

First Floor . . . 754 sq. ft.

14

Modern version of traditional salt box

PLAN 2720

The sloping rear roof line of this Colonial salt box is echoed in the garage design. Shuttered windows, paneled entrance door with flanking sidelights and bay windows complement the authentic exterior styling. Gracefully turned Colonial posts accent the living room doorways between the foyer and dining area. Downstairs, the master bedroom boasts a large walk-in closet and full private bath. The second floor offers three bedrooms, storage areas and two baths. Material list is included and mirror reverse plans are available at no additional cost if specified.

Designer: Henry D. Norris, AIA

First Floor . . . 2075 sq. ft.

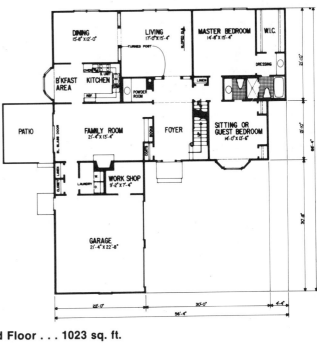

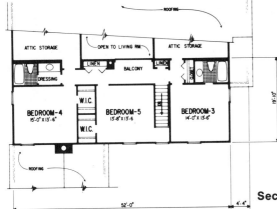

Second Floor . . . 1023 sq. ft.

15

Compact charmer features options

PLAN 4315

Rustic board and batten exterior siding, cross-buck door with sidelights, and second story dormer windows provide the authentic detailing on this Early American home. The uncluttered first floor plan concentrates living space in the large activity room and country kitchen. The standard four bedroom, two bath plan has a basement and an optional spacious master bedroom layout with extra storage and powder rooms. Complete materials list is available for an additional $10, and mirror reverse plans are available if specified.

Designer: W. D. Farmer

First Floor . . . 1029 sq. ft.
Second Floor . . . 548 sq. ft.

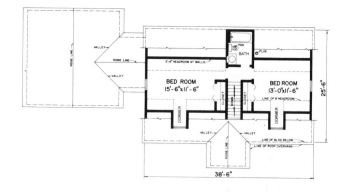

Alternate one bedroom

Large Colonial offers separate unit

PLAN 5905

This sprawling Colonial home with two-story front porch and large covered side patio is designed to accommodate a large family. With six bedrooms on the second floor, the private bedroom over the garage area can be used as an in-law apartment or maid's room. The rear stair makes this area accessible without affecting the main house. Located at the rear of the first floor, the study can double as a guest bedroom when additional sleeping space is needed. Mirror reverse plans are available if specified at no extra cost, and materials list is included.

Designer: Evan Pollitt, Architect

Second Floor . . . 2056 sq. ft.

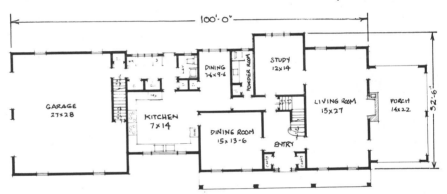

TO ORDER
BUILDING BLUEPRINTS
USE ORDER FORM
ON PAGE 111

First Floor . . . 1650 sq. ft.
Basement . . . 1650 sq. ft.

B. NATHAN

Colonial charm on two floors

PLAN 4212

Exterior architectural detailing of this home includes a second story overhang, and arched porch supports between house and garage which is repeated in the arched garage doors. The charming foyer with graceful stairway leads to a large master bedroom with dressing area and private bath plus three additional bedrooms. The first floor offers a generous living room and kitchen with nearby family room where the large fireplace is flanked with floor-to-ceiling bookcases. Mirror reverse plans are available if specified at no additional cost.

Designer: Claude Miquelle Associates

TO ORDER
BUILDING BLUEPRINTS
USE ORDER FORM
ON PAGE 111

First Floor . . . 1124 sq. ft.
Second Floor . . . 918 sq. ft.

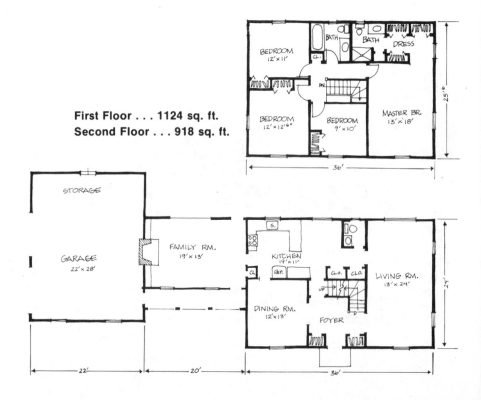

Country Colonial designed for privacy

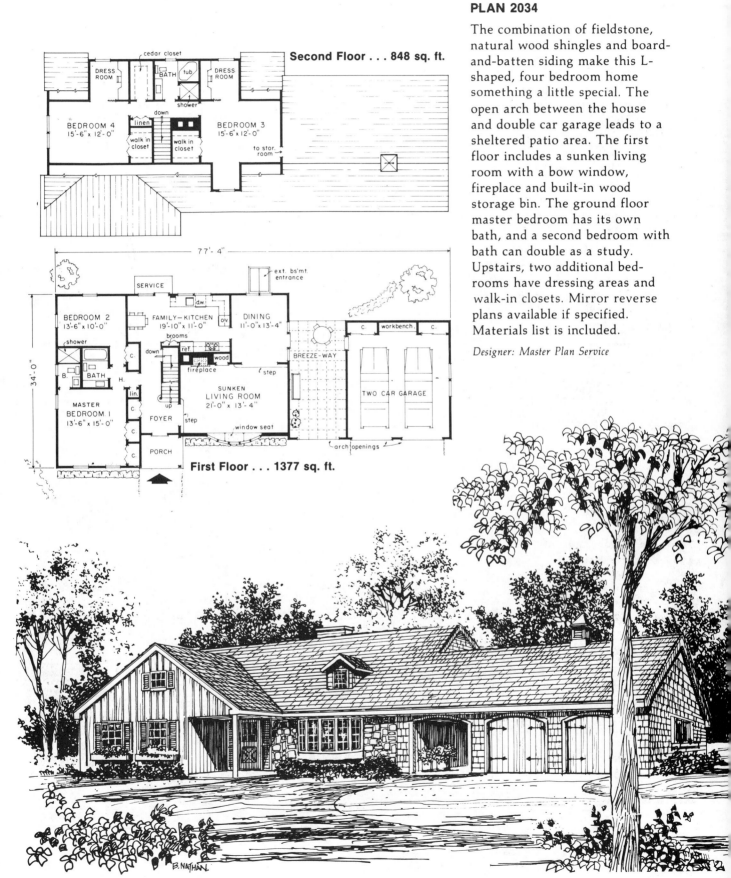

Second Floor . . . 848 sq. ft.

DRESS ROOM

cedar closet

BATH | tub

DRESS ROOM

shower

BEDROOM 4
15'-6" x 12'-0"

linen | down

walk in closet | walk in closet

BEDROOM 3
15'-6" x 12'-0"

to stor. room

PLAN 2034

The combination of fieldstone, natural wood shingles and board-and-batten siding make this L-shaped, four bedroom home something a little special. The open arch between the house and double car garage leads to a sheltered patio area. The first floor includes a sunken living room with a bow window, fireplace and built-in wood storage bin. The ground floor master bedroom has its own bath, and a second bedroom with bath can double as a study. Upstairs, two additional bedrooms have dressing areas and walk-in closets. Mirror reverse plans available if specified. Materials list is included.

Designer: Master Plan Service

77'-4"

SERVICE

ext. bs'mt. entrance

BEDROOM 2
13'-6" x 10'-0"

FAMILY—KITCHEN
19'-10" x 11'-0"

DINING
11'-0" x 13'-4"

shower

dw.

ov.

brooms

down | ref. | wood

34'-0"

B. | BATH

fireplace

step

MASTER BEDROOM 1
13'-6" x 15'-0"

up

lin.

SUNKEN LIVING ROOM
21'-0" x 13'-4"

BREEZE-WAY

workbench

c. | c.

TWO CAR GARAGE

FOYER

step

window seat

PORCH

arch openings

First Floor . . . 1377 sq. ft.

B. NATHAN.

Traditional exterior of brick and wood

PLAN 3323

A tasteful blend of siding materials sets this home apart. The main structure has brick facing below the gambrel roof, and a classic paneled door illuminated by two brass coach lamps. The garage and family room portion is sided with board and batten stained to harmonize with the adjoining brick. The interior plan features four bedrooms and three baths, formal dining room, large kitchen and adjoining family room with a large fireplace. Mirror reverse plans available if specified; materials list available for an extra $10. Please specify optional foundations: slab, crawl space or full basement.

Designer: W. L. Corley

TO ORDER
BUILDING BLUEPRINTS
USE ORDER FORM
ON PAGE 111

Second Floor . . . 930 sq. ft.

First Floor . . . 1430 sq. ft.

20

Add-on becomes authentic salt box

PLAN 5906

A Colonial plan, based on the West Hartford, Connecticut home where Noah Webster was born, reflects a typical early architectural practice. The rear portion of the house was added later transforming the original design into a salt box profile. The unusually large kitchen with U-shaped layout has a fireplace with built-in grille. A laundry, lavatory and pantry lie between house and garage. The plan includes one bedroom and bath on the lower level, with two bedrooms, bath and storage on the second floor. Materials list included; mirror reverse plans available if specified.

Designer: Evan Pollitt, Architect

Second Floor . . . 770 sq. ft.

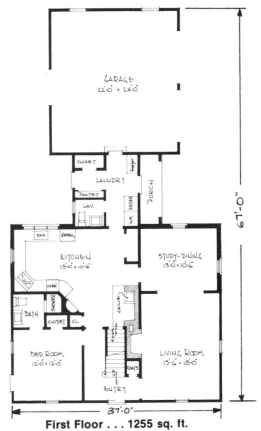

First Floor . . . 1255 sq. ft.
Basement . . . 1255 sq. ft.

Two-story Southern Colonial styled after Mount Vernon

PLAN 2318

Styled after George Washington's home in Mount Vernon, this two-story house has the grace and charm associated with Southern Colonial design. The elegant columns and symmetrical front facade set off the broken scroll pediment doorway. The central foyer has the dining room on one side, sunken living room on the other and the family room and kitchen in the rear. On the second floor, there are four bedrooms and two baths. The house may be built with a full basement or on a slab. Materials list is included. Mirror reverse plans are available for $10 additional.

Designer: Samuel Paul, AIA

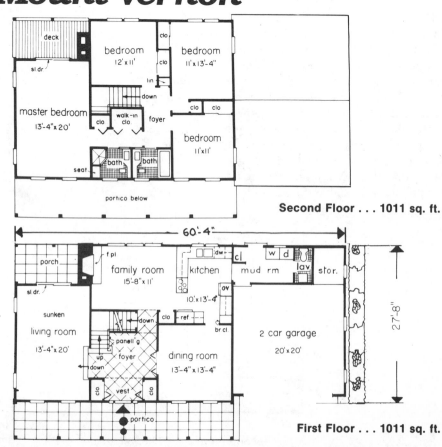

Second Floor . . . 1011 sq. ft.

First Floor . . . 1011 sq. ft.

Rustic Cape Cod features garage loft

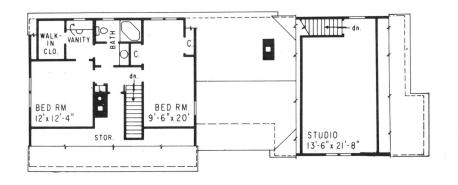

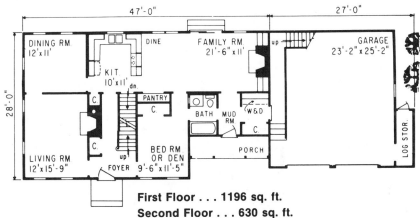

First Floor . . . 1196 sq. ft.
Second Floor . . . 630 sq. ft.
Garage Loft . . . 364 sq. ft.

PLAN 2241

Special features are designed into this compact home. An exceptionally large country kitchen-family room has an old fashioned pantry and fireplace. The first floor offers a den or guest bedroom with full bath, formal living room, dining room, laundry and garage access. Two charming bedrooms, large closets and bath complete the upstairs. Huge loft over the garage is ideal as a studio, hobby area or extra guest room. A handy firewood storage area is tucked under the side of the garage. Material list is included; full reverse plans cost $30 extra.

Designer: National Plan Service

TO ORDER
BUILDING BLUEPRINTS
USE ORDER FORM
ON PAGE 111

Spacious home in southland image

PLAN 4311

This impressive two-story structure, while reminiscent of slower-paced life in the Old South, is practically geared for today's living. First floor includes a bedroom and full bath, great for overnight guests. Family room has a sloped ceiling and fireplace, and easy access to outdoors. Three bedrooms, one with its own sitting area, occupy space on the second level along with two full baths. Mirror reverse plans available if specified; materials list is an additional $10.

Designer: W. D. Farmer

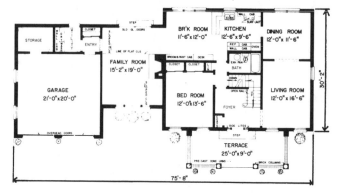

Lower Level . . . 1452 sq. ft.

TO ORDER
BUILDING BLUEPRINTS
USE ORDER FORM
ON PAGE 111

Upper Level . . . 1147 sq. ft.

Salt box features open, easy-flow interiors

PLAN 2402

Each floor has its own complete bath in this surprisingly spacious three bedroom house. Master bedroom is tucked in front corner of the house. Staircase towards the back of the home gives second-story early risers direct access to the kitchen, while a bunk area off the living room provides sleep space for guests. Electrical layouts are provided on the plan, which meet most states' requirements. Materials list is included. Mirror reverse plans available if specified.

Designer: William M. Thompson, AIA

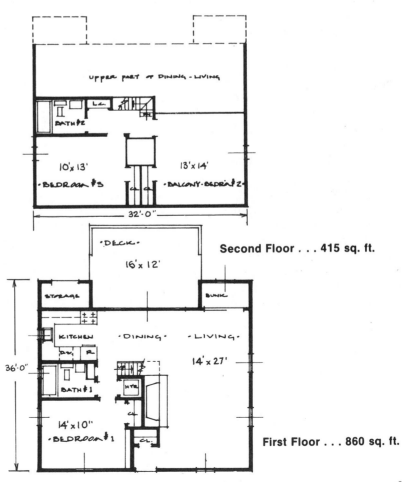

UPPER PART OF DINING - LIVING

BATH #2

10' x 13'
·BEDROOM #3·

13' x 14'
·BALCONY·BEDROOM 2·

32'-0"

Second Floor . . . 415 sq. ft.

·DECK·
16' x 12'

STORAGE

BUNK

KITCHEN

·DINING·

·LIVING·
14' x 27'

36'-0"

BATH #1

14' x 10"
·BEDROOM #1·

First Floor . . . 860 sq. ft.

Colonial millwork adds special touch

PLAN 4316

In the entrance foyer of this home, the tone is established by the traditional styled newell posts and turned stairway balusters. To the right, the large activity room with fireplace continues the theme with decoratively turned spindles topping a half partition wall. The spacious kitchen with adjacent breakfast area leads directly to the formal dining room. First floor master bedroom contains walk-in closet, bath and dressing room. Upstairs, two large bedrooms share a full bath. Mirror reverse plans are available at no cost if specified. Materials list available for an additional $10.

Designer: W. D. Farmer

TO ORDER
BUILDING BLUEPRINTS
USE ORDER FORM
ON PAGE 111

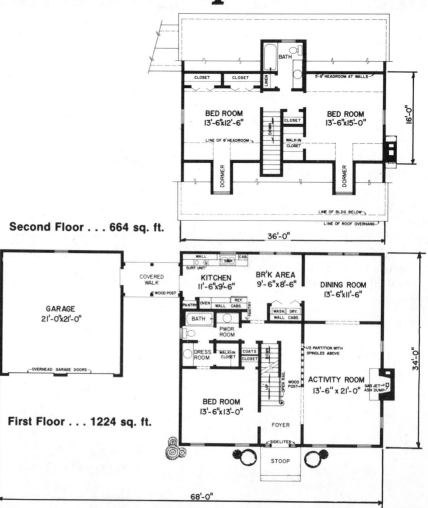

Second Floor . . . 664 sq. ft.

First Floor . . . 1224 sq. ft.

Exterior design retains overhang

PLAN 2409

Early American construction methods often include an overhanging second story. Here, the overhanging front facade is accented with four hanging drops or "pendills" to complement the narrow siding and shuttered windows. A gracious entry hall leads up the stairway to four bedrooms and two complete baths on the second story. The main floor has a large family room off the U-shaped kitchen layout, formal dining room and spacious living room with central fireplace. Mirror reverse plans available at no additional cost if specified. Materials list is included.

Designer: William M. Thompson, AIA

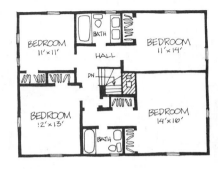

Second Floor . . . 936 sq. ft.

First Floor . . . 1130 sq. ft.

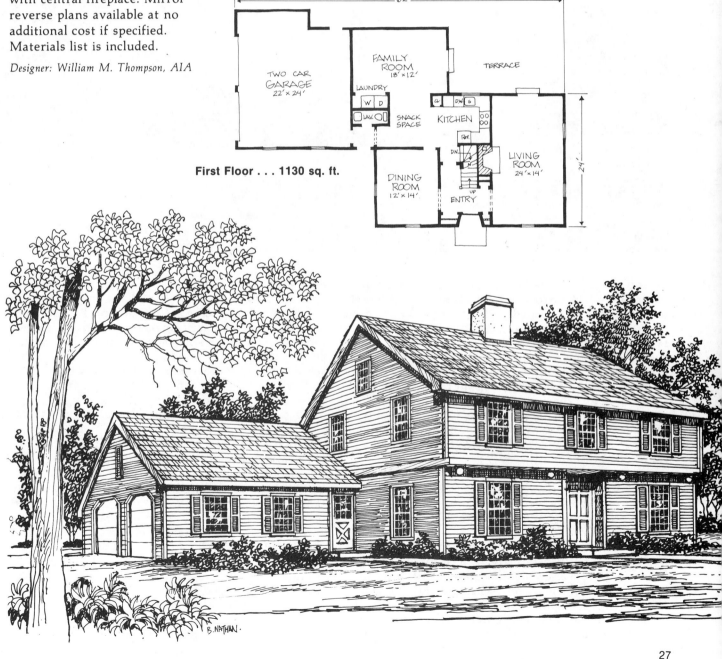

B. NATHAN.

Evolution of Early American Architecture

Early Colonial America represented a most unique period in world history. Architecturally, the period has never been duplicated. For within the short span of 100 years, five or six distinct but interrelated residential housing styles were developed, and their continued popularity today justifies the validity of their practical and aesthetic design. The variety can be partially explained by the European roots of the new settlers. Both French and Dutch influences are discernable with the English styling predominating. But the speed and sureness of this architectural revolution requires a closer look at the historical factors which spawned the changes.

SKILLED ARTISANS
The early colonists were a special breed. Obviously, they were not the poor farmer or shop clerk, since this class could not afford the cost of passage to the new country. Nor were they the landed gentry or prosperous merchant, since this group, already well established in Europe, saw no advantage in risking their future in an untried land. What did arrive on our shores was a talented and ambitious group who sought both religious and economic freedom. They felt trapped in the middle strata of European society

and were willing to risk what they had for the opportunity to use their talents. The court records of the New Haven Colony, for instance, list "sawyers, joyners, thatchers, brickmakers, plasterers, carpenters, ryvers of clapboards, shingles and lathes, naylers and massons." Those who were not farmers had served long apprenticeships in the European tradition and, without hope of establishing their own business, these highly specialized and skillfully trained individuals fled their home country for a new start.

TRADITION PLUS ADAPTATION
Early craftsmen attempted to duplicate the homes they had left behind. The English colonists, trying to build their traditional English cottage with its thatched roof and timbered framework filled in with masonry or stonework, ran into immediate problems. A thatched roof in England's relatively mild but damp climate worked well, but the harsh New England coastline with its raging winter storms and long, dry summers, forced a re-evaluation. After several disastrous fires, thatched roofs were banned. Native stone was abundant in the colonies as any farmer, cursing and sweating as he dislodged stone after boulder from his plowed field and piled them in fence rows, could

Photography: James Brett

WHAT IS STYLE?

Before examining various Colonial styles, it might be helpful to get a professional's definition of the term "style." Architect Claude Miquelle, long associated with traditional Colonial design, states, "When we say of a home that 'It has style', we mean it has class or distinction. Style is also a collection of handles by which the various regional architectures are described. Each one has a set of distinguishing characteristics peculiar to it. There will be a combination of elements of proportion, textures, details and colors in a given setting. Generally speaking, all of these must be present in sufficient degree and mixture to make the

attest. However, lime, a key ingredient in producing mortar, was scarce. The few small natural lime deposits and the lime manufactured from crushed seashells was used where it was most important — for chimney construction. Yet the new land was heavily timbered and wood roof shingles and siding material were cheap and highy serviceable. But traditions die hard. With all the tall white pine available in the East, the colonial housebuilder still preferred to construct his frames from the dense and therefore heavier and harder to work with oak timbers.

And thus the original "Colonial style" home began to take shape. The floor plan was an efficient square or rectangle with no tricky setbacks or expensive angles. The home was set solidly on the ground with a heavy post and girt frame construction with lighter vertical studs between the posts. The core was a massive stone chimney and the home was literally built around the masonry which often contained several fireplaces. Even the smaller homes were usually two story to gain full living space from the foundation. A steeply pitched, shingled roof and narrow clapboard siding provided a weatherproof exterior. Since imported glass was expensive, windows were few but well placed to give some light to each room. By today's standards, the home was for the most part drafty, cold in the winter, hot during the summer and poorly lit, yet, for the times, no European monarch lived more comfortably or heartily than the average hardworking American colonist. Through ingenuity and simple construction methods, they were able to adapt the materials at hand.

design come off right and be authentic. Such things as heights, roof pitch, siding, details of doors and windows, and colors are the features which distinguish the various styles, such as the early New England salt box." Miquelle then sums it up with, "Good design usually employs simple materials, avoids gimmicks. Authenticity is the key to good traditional design."

COLONIAL 1690-1760

The photo to the left and the illustration above represent what most people think of as a typical early Colonial structure. It is characterized by the two-story, square design dominated by the large central chimney. The steeply pitched roof is shingled and the narrow siding is finished with simple corner boards. Today's siding is usually exposed six or eight inches to the weather, but the true New England colonial calls for clapboards four inches to the weather. The facade is relatively plain with minimum and simple frames around the door and windows. Window glass was at first imported and therefore expensive. The small pane size, generally six by eight inches, was usually set in wood sash in either an 8 over 12 or 12 over 12 pattern. Over the entrance door, small panes of glass were often used. Because of the height, light rather than visibility was required, so often cheaper "bullseye" glass, wavy and difficult to see through, was used. The early style was symmetrical with one or two windows on either side of the door, matched by three or five windows in the second story. Few have survived without the addition of wings and lean-tos.

continued

Early American Architecture

GARRISON 1640-1700

Pre-dating the typical "Colonial" styling were two distinctly different designs which, with modification in line and material, were later to reappear as more modern Colonial styles. The first of these, the Garrison home, is characterized by the front overhang of the second story. Like the typical Colonial, the Garrison found most frequently in the seacoast settlements of Plymouth, Boston and Salem, was strictly English in heritage. This earliest of Colonials had the large central chimney, steep roof line and narrow clapboard siding, but the lines and proportions were much more crude than later models. The entrance door was usually two layers of rough hewn planks nailed at right angles for strength, and the few small windows were set very high on the wall, more for illumination and security than visibility. The second story front overhang characteristic, often extending up to two feet beyond the first floor wall, has generated several explanations. Some historians and writers have romanticized that the early settlers needed peep holes from which they could peer down at the lower walls of their homes to see wild animals, strangers and marauding Indians that might threaten their security. Unfortunately, this colorful theory does not hold up when on closer inspection, few if any such peep holes are found in Garrison homes. However, if you start your speculation on the proven assumption that the Colonial builder was at heart a practical craftsman, then a more reasonable explanation evolves. In making the transition from the English Tudor half-timbered house to the New England braced frame construction, the front overhang was retained. Originally, the English home was built in two steps with the larger second story sitting on top of the first story framework. In the Colonial braced frame version, the rear posts were carried up the full two stories in one piece and the front posts were cut off at the second floor level to provide for the overhang. The weight of the overhang, cantilevered on the vertical post, tended to

bend the beam upward stiffening and eliminating sag, allowing a lighter member to be used. Later, when a large interior beam, called the summer beam was introduced, the need for the overhang with its carved

drops or "pendills" was eliminated, and by 1700 the overhang in American architecture had disappeared.

DUTCH COLONIAL 1640-1720

At approximately the same period as the Garrison was developed by the English, Dutch and Flemish settlers in New Amsterdam, and along the Hudson and Mohawk River valleys of early New York, adapted their own distinctive style. The Dutch Colonial home was generally an urban rather than farm structure. The good burghers were, by tradition merchants and not tillers of the soil. Their city homes were generally two-story brick rather than clapboard, with steep pitched

roofs and straight-sided gables topped by chimneys at both ends. Clay lugs or tile usually covered the roof rather than wood shingles. To the Dutch, a brick home was a sign of wealth, and only farmers and tradesmen lived in a stone or wooden home. In rural areas, the broad gambreled roof characterized the majority of Dutch Colonial homes.

SALT BOX 1700-1770

Salt was a familiar ingredient used often by the Colonial housewife. Not only did it season food but, more importantly, it was used as a preservative. With no modern refrigeration, meat and fish were liberally coated with salt to retard spoilage. Anyone fortunate enough to have enjoyed a cod fish cake dinner in a good Boston restaurant can appreciate the amount of salt used daily by early housewives. The ever-present salt box in the Colonial kitchen had a peaked top with a liftable front lid. The "Salt Box" home, with its distinctive roof line, actually developed in 16th and 17th century England but was popularized in the Colonies. It evolved from the practice of adding a lean-to on the rear of a conventional two-story, peaked roof home. As families grew and more space was needed, rooms were added in the first floor rear and the original roof line was carried down over the addition in one continuous sweep. This gave the home the silhouette of the old salt box. Sometimes a change in the angle of

the back roof shows where the lean-to was added. The addition usually enclosed a kitchen, pantry and borning room. As time progressed, the design became so popular that houses were built with the long back roof as part of the original structure.

CAPE COD 1710-1830

The compact Cape Cod home represents Colonial construction at its most practical. It's a regional adaptation perfectly suited to the area. Cape Cod Peninsular, like an arm reaching from Massachusetts back toward England, is exposed to the full fury of the North Atlantic storms. The first settlers from Devon and Cornwall in the west of England, adapted their traditional small cottages to meet the elements of the new land. The low story-and-one-half-high framed structure is set close to the ground. The long, low roof, reaching down to the top of the windows and door, is relatively flat with a typical 8/12 pitch. A large central chimney and no dormers distinguishes the roofline. To increase attic headroom, builders sometimes used a bowed or "rainbow" roof construction similar to the curved hull of a ship. The original Cape Cods were covered on the roof and all sides with wood shingles that were allowed to weather a pewter gray, with later houses sided in clapboard. This was the expandable house with three basic designs; half house — two windows to one side of the front door; three-quarters house — two windows to one side of the door and one on the other; and the full Cape Cod, symmetrically designed with two windows to either side of the door.

EARLY GEORGIAN 1720-1760

Up to this point in Colonial architecture, the designs had been simple and practical. The Garrison, Dutch and English Colonial, Salt Box and Cap Cod styling was produced by agreement between the owner and a local craftsman who drew on personal knowledge of designs from the mother country or those they saw around them. However, the Early Georgian homes introduced an outside element into styling. The professional architect, rather than the builder/owner began to influence design. As the new country prospered, the affluent tired of the plain and homespun styles and reached out for something dramatically new. Georgian architecture took its name from the 18th century kings of England, but its design reached back through 16th century Italian Renaissance to the classical Roman details and proportions. The home was set on a high foundation and emphasized the ornate entrance in the middle of the house. The wide paneled door had a row of rectangular lights or transom lights above. Detailed columns or fluted pilasters often framed the door, with ornate pediments above. The plain Colonial eves were replaced with a cornice, often with classical features such as dentil moulding. When dormers were used, they had triangular pediments and were symmetrically spaced. Rooflines were usually pitched or sometimes hipped; siding material was usually brick, stone or

wood. The symmetrical design was carried out with twin chimneys at either end of the rectangular two-story house, and shutters framed the even numbered windows on the ground floor and the odd numbered ones on the second story.

The various Colonial home styles developed in that brief 100 year period have remained popular for several hundred years and show no signs of decreasing in the future. In fact, the trend seems to be growing, and with good reason. These homes offer both a touch of nostalgia and some very practical answers to today's living. Many today feel disconnected from their heritage, and a Colonial home provides a sense of roots.

All dates approximate. Colonial, Salt Box, Cape Cod and Early Georgian drawings are from A Field Guide to Old-House Styles, *published by "The Old-House Journal."*

Early American "add-on" look

PLAN 2035

The main two-story gambrel roof section of this home is angled away from the garage wing. On the exterior, barn-like arched openings form a small entrance veranda and continue across the garage doors. On the interior, the foyer opens on one side to a pleasant living room with a large bowed window. On the other side, there's a spacious kitchen-family room layout. The curved staircase sweeps upward to a master suite with dressing area and bath, and two other bedrooms and bath. Materials list included, mirror reverse plans available if specified at no extra cost.

Designer: Master Plan Service

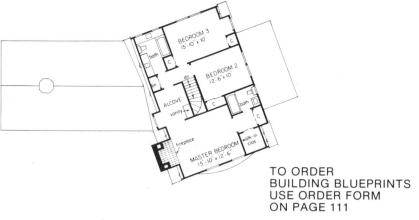

TO ORDER
BUILDING BLUEPRINTS
USE ORDER FORM
ON PAGE 111

First Floor . . . 1156 sq. ft.
Second Floor . . . 881 sq. ft.

Economical 1½-story contains four bedrooms

PLAN 2324
PLAN 2324-A (without basement)

The low eve line, unbroken high pitched roof, double hung windows, narrow wood siding and slatted shutters of this home all belong to the traditional Cape Cod style. Compact yet surprisingly spacious, the first floor features living room with fireplace, dining room, kitchen with dining area plus two bedrooms and bath. Second floor space in the roof area has two bedrooms and bath. The home may be constructed with a full basement or on a slab foundation. Materials list included; mirror reverse plans available for $10 extra.

Designer: Samuel Paul, AIA

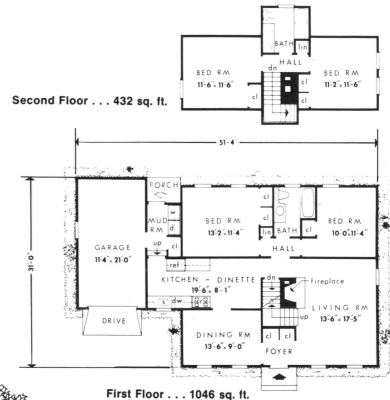

Second Floor . . . 432 sq. ft.

First Floor . . . 1046 sq. ft.

Wrought iron lamps highlight entrances

PLAN 4207

Careful attention to detail, traditional materials and classic proportions mark this two-story colonial exterior. The living room with fireplace runs the full depth of the home. First floor plan includes lavatory, laundry room, U-shaped kitchen, half wall between dinette and family room, and dining room. Four bedrooms and two baths complete the second level. The plan is ideal for a sloping lot with the garage tucked under the first floor family room. Mirror reverse plans are available at no additional cost when specified.

Designer: Claude Miquelle Associates

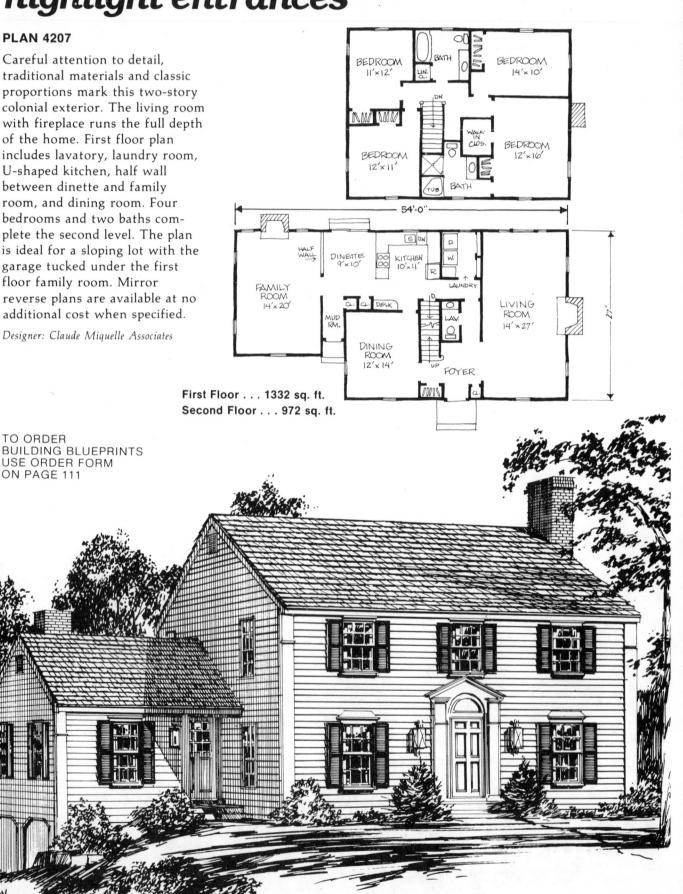

First Floor . . . 1332 sq. ft.
Second Floor . . . 972 sq. ft.

TO ORDER
BUILDING BLUEPRINTS
USE ORDER FORM
ON PAGE 111

Outdoor living adds extra space

PLAN 2036

This lovely two-story home in Early American design offers a large flagstone rear porch with a spacious second story deck for extra livability. Room-size natural stone foyer with winding staircase has a dining room on one side with front to rear living room on the other. Utility room, typical of an Early American pantry, includes the laundry, a lavatory, service and garage door and stair to basement. Second floor provides four bedrooms and two baths. Materials list is included and mirror reverse plans are available at no additional cost if specified.

Designer: Master Plan Service

First Floor . . . 1281 sq. ft.
Second Floor . . . 979 sq. ft.

Cape Cod design, modern and traditional

PLAN 3519

The ageless charm of the Cape Cod design with its dormer windows, louver shutters and symmetrical lines has remained popular over the years. From the entry, the stairway leads up to the second floor and two bedrooms and a bath. On the main level the spacious living-dining area extends from the front to the rear of the home. The long, narrow kitchen contains an eating nook and washer/dryer plus storage space in the utility room. Den or bedroom with bath complete the plan. Mirror reverse plans available if specified for an additional $5.

Designer: Hiawatha Estes & Assoc.

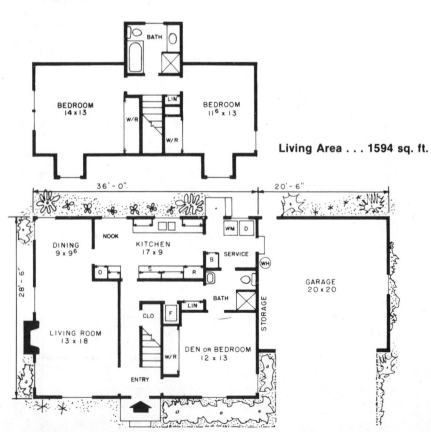

Living Area . . . 1594 sq. ft.

Unique roofline blends early styling

PLAN 2410

Three second-story window dormers establish the gambrel design of the front roofline of this home, while the rear roof adopts a modified salt box slant. The traditionally proportioned exterior allows the horizontal shingle lines to blend with the narrow wood siding and garage door sections. The first floor includes a large living room, dining room, family room with fireplace and snack area next to the kitchen. A lavatory and laundry room are off the entry hall. Upstairs there are four bedrooms and two baths. Mirror reverse plans are available if specified.

Designer: William M. Thompson, AIA

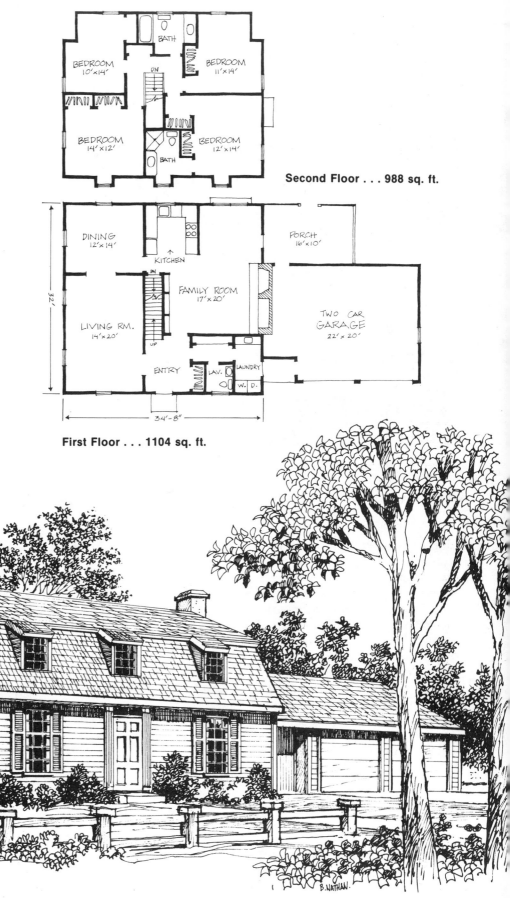

Second Floor . . . 988 sq. ft.

BEDROOM 10'x14'

BEDROOM 11'x14'

BATH

DN

BEDROOM 14'x12'

BATH

BEDROOM 12'x14'

DINING 12'x14'

KITCHEN

PORCH 16'x10'

FAMILY ROOM 17'x20'

TWO CAR GARAGE 22'x20'

LIVING RM. 14'x20'

DN

UP

ENTRY

LAV.

LAUNDRY

W. D.

32'

34'-8"

First Floor . . . 1104 sq. ft.

TO ORDER
BUILDING BLUEPRINTS
USE ORDER FORM
ON PAGE 111

B. NATHAN.

Well-balanced
New England cottage design

PLAN 5907

In Colonial construction, traditionally the center section with central chimney and small dormer window in the gambrel room was built first. Later, wings were added at various times without destroying the charming proportions. The home shown here has a large bookcase-lined living room and fireplace, and pantry between the kitchen and dining room on the first floor. Upstairs are two bedrooms, bath and study, plus a future bedroom over the two car garage. The materials list for this 17th century cottage is included. Mirror reverse plans are available at no extra cost if specified.

Designer: Evan Pollitt, Architect

TO ORDER
BUILDING BLUEPRINTS
USE ORDER FORM
ON PAGE 111

Second Floor . . . 712 sq. ft.

First Floor . . . 1115 sq. ft.
Basement . . . 1115 sq. ft.

Salt box is compact and comfortable

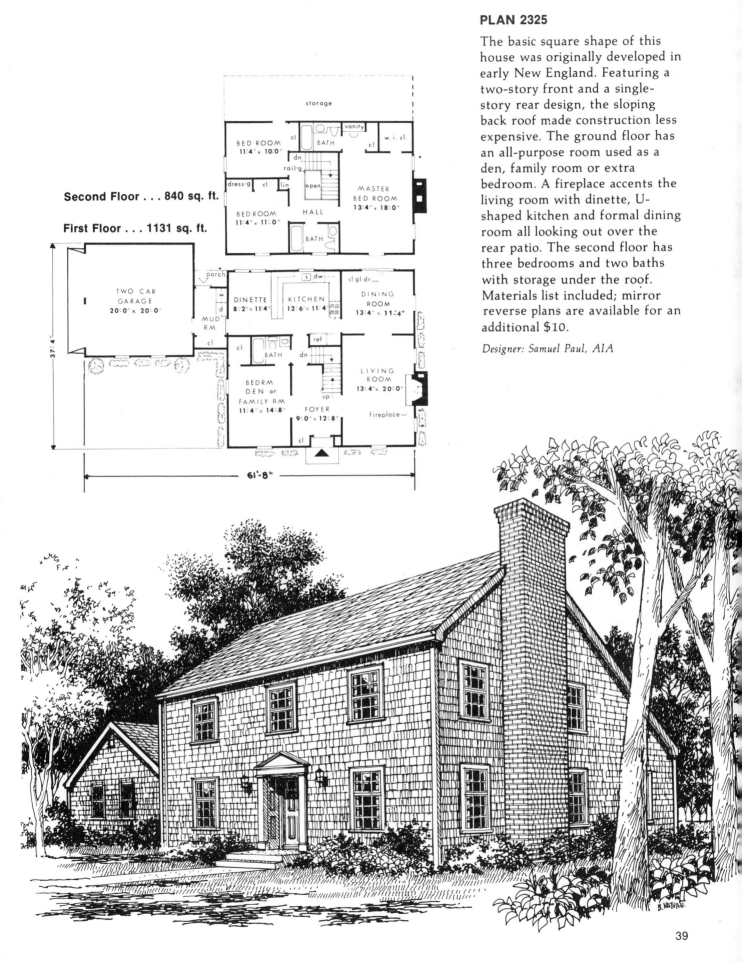

Second Floor . . . 840 sq. ft.

First Floor . . . 1131 sq. ft.

PLAN 2325

The basic square shape of this house was originally developed in early New England. Featuring a two-story front and a single-story rear design, the sloping back roof made construction less expensive. The ground floor has an all-purpose room used as a den, family room or extra bedroom. A fireplace accents the living room with dinette, U-shaped kitchen and formal dining room all looking out over the rear patio. The second floor has three bedrooms and two baths with storage under the roof. Materials list included; mirror reverse plans are available for an additional $10.

Designer: Samuel Paul, AIA

Broken facade projects shadow lines

PLAN 3324

This architect has taken traditional Colonial design components and arranged them in three sections to create an interesting interplay of light and shadow. On the left, the main section of the house features a bay window in the dining room. The family room in the center is dominated by one wall of bookcases. Master bedroom is downstairs, two bedrooms, bath and study upstairs. When ordering, please specify foundation options: slab, crawl space or basement. Mirror reverse plans available if specified at no charge; materials list available for $10 extra.

Designer: W. L. Corley

Second Floor . . . 765 sq. ft.

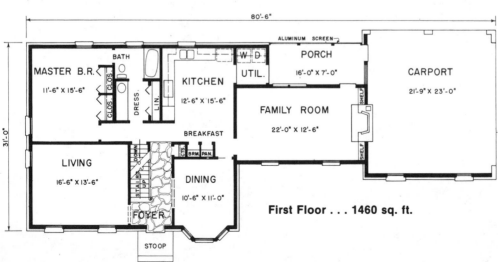

First Floor . . . 1460 sq. ft.

Two-story Colonial has balanced design

PLAN 4317

The handsome exterior of this home features extra tall windows, paneled front door with flanking sidelights and ornate broken pediment entrance. Wrought iron railings and overhead coach lantern complete the traditional look. Brick wings to either side contain two bedrooms and two baths with double carport, utility room and storage on the other side. Large family room on first floor has fireplace and open ceiling construction. Second floor has two bedrooms and bath. Materials list costs an additional $10. Mirror reverse plans are available if specified at no extra cost.

Designer: W. D. Farmer

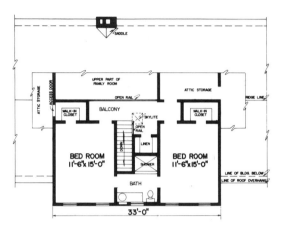

Second Floor . . . 660 sq. ft.

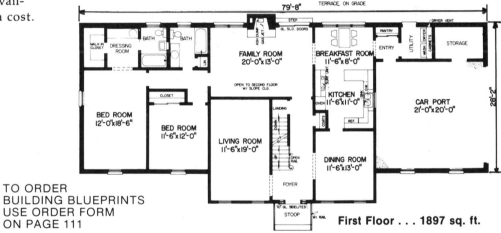

First Floor . . . 1897 sq. ft.

TO ORDER
BUILDING BLUEPRINTS
USE ORDER FORM
ON PAGE 111

41

Angled design creates interest

PLAN 4208

By offsetting the two car garage on the left, the architect was able to achieve the random add-on look associated with early Colonial construction. A covered walk with angled timber supports leads from the garage area past the family room to the main house with overhanging second story and decorative drop pediments. Spacious first floor plan contains living room, dining room, large kitchen, breakfast area and lavatory. Four bedrooms and two baths complete the second story. Mirror reverse plans are available if specified at no additional cost.

Designer: Claude Miquelle Associates

Second Floor . . . 895 sq. ft.

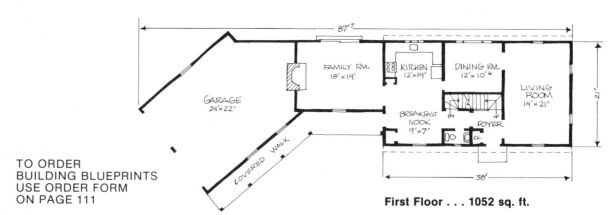

TO ORDER
BUILDING BLUEPRINTS
USE ORDER FORM
ON PAGE 111

First Floor . . . 1052 sq. ft.

Master bedroom has private fireplace

PLAN 2721

The ground hugging design of this large Colonial home gives it a feeling of solid comfort. The first floor plan offers exceptionally large rooms throughout — spacious kitchen and breakfast area, formal dining room, living room and oversize family room with fireplace. The ground level master bedroom has a private bath, walk-in closet and features an individual fireplace in the corner. Upstairs are two huge bedrooms, bath and an unusual amount of storage. Materials list is included and mirror reverse plans are available if specified at no extra cost.

Designer: Henry D. Norris, AIA

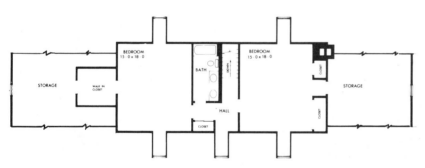

Second Floor . . . 900 sq. ft.

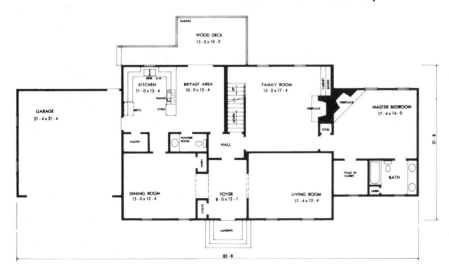

First Floor . . . 1780 sq. ft.

Gambrel roof identifies Dutch Colonial

PLAN 2326

The double slope of this gambrel roof design allows more space to be utilized on the second floor than is possible with a conventional single sloped roof line. Dormers, overhanging second story, window and door shutters give a solid feeling to the exterior. The first floor plan revolves around a central foyer and both family and living room lead to a rear covered porch. Pantry, mud room and breakfast areas are adjacent to the kitchen. Four bedrooms and two baths make up the second floor. Plans include materials list; mirror reverse plans are available if specified for an additional $10.

Designer: Samuel Paul, AIA

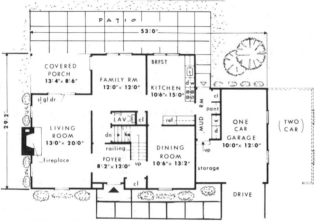

TO ORDER
BUILDING BLUEPRINTS
USE ORDER FORM
ON PAGE 111

First Floor . . . 956 sq. ft.
Second Floor . . . 1007 sq. ft.

Simple design features expandable plan

Second Floor . . . 720 sq. ft.

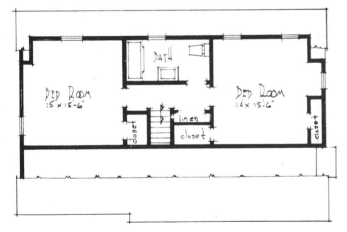

PLAN 5908

Here is a compact Cape Cod-style home perfect for the young married couple. Two large bedrooms and bath on the second floor can be completed later as additional space becomes necessary for a growing family. The first floor plan offers complete living space for a new family with two large bedrooms and bath plus a generous living room complete with bookcase-lined fireplace. The spacious U-shaped kitchen has a handy utility area and the nearby dining space features two built-in corner china closets. Materials list included, and mirror reverse plans are available if specified at no extra cost.

Designer: Evan Pollitt, Architect

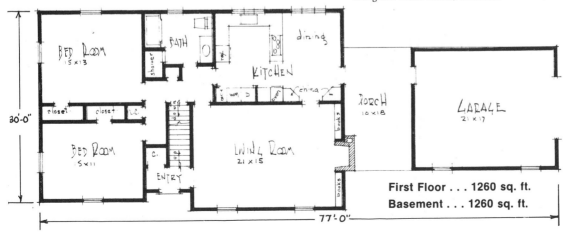

First Floor . . . 1260 sq. ft.
Basement . . . 1260 sq. ft.

Early American added-on appearance

PLAN 2037

With the center section of fieldstone and the side wings of wooden clapboard, the exterior of this one-story home re-states the Early American added-on look — as families grew in size, rooms were constructed from the most readily available materials. The floor plan includes three bedrooms, two baths and a lavatory, living room with fireplace and family room opening onto the covered flagstone patio. The laundry room and pantry are directly off the large kitchen. A two car garage has interior closets. Mirror reverse plans available if specified and materials list is included.

Designer: Master Plan Service

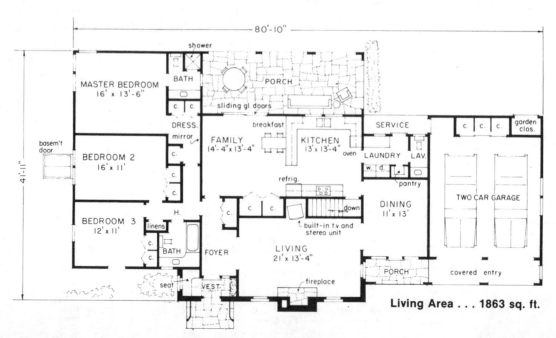

Living Area . . . 1863 sq. ft.

Stately Colonial accents exterior millwork

PLAN 4318

This two-story Colonial home captures the traditional look of the period through careful use of exterior ornamentation — wide corner boards, painted a contrasting color, framing the facade with its dentil mouldings at the eve line, railed fence atop the columned porch sheltering the paneled entrance door with leaded glass sidelights. Decorative millwork crowning the first story shuttered windows heightens the effect. Highly livable floor plan includes four bedrooms and two-and-one-half baths. Materials list available for an additional $10. Mirror reverse plans available if specified at no additional cost.

Designer: W. D. Farmer

TO ORDER
BUILDING BLUEPRINTS
USE ORDER FORM
ON PAGE 111

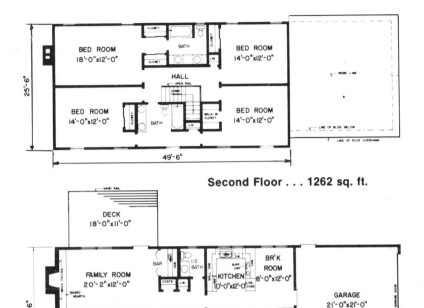

Second Floor . . . 1262 sq. ft.

First Floor . . . 1262 sq. ft.

Photography: John Hartley

The Colonial Kitchen...Today

The phrase "hearth and home" conjures up a Colonial family scene with children playing before the open fireplace while the womenfolk prepare the evening meal and the men, after a hard day in the fields and barn, mend a broken harness or fashion a wooden stool for the newest family member. It is a cozy atmosphere, with the flickering fire casting warmth and shadows about the room filled with the odors of cooking food, spices, well handled leather and the sounds of a busy family preparing for the evening meal as dripping fat, popping and sputtering, falls from the cooking meat to the flames below. Yet we forget that the Colonial kitchen of the 17th century was poorly lit, drafty, water was carried by the bucketful and the wide fireplace consumed huge quantities of fuel which had to be replaced hourly. The Colonial kitchen of today is not a museum reproduction but a modern, efficient setting that recaptures the warmth and family solidarity of earlier days without neglecting the step-saving conveniences so necessary in today's more hectic living. It's a careful blend of the old, the old looking and the most modern. Natural materials play a big part in setting the proper atmosphere. Rough beamed ceilings, wood wall paneling and cabinetry, stone and brick, wrought iron, brass and copper utensils and both bright and subtle fabric patterns. Colors are usually based on earth tones with splashes of warmer and livelier shades as accents. Lighting may feature Colonial wall or ceiling fixtures with an assist from more modern illumination. Appliances, sometimes built-in, sometimes free-standing, are selected for color compatibility as much as for efficiency. Finishes today range from dark brown and chocolate to rust and copper tones. Even a microwave oven can look comfortable in a traditional setting. Furniture is usually natural wood or upholstered in durable open weave fabrics but the styling is always clean, simple and honest. Jointery techniques are accented rather than hidden so trestle table wedges and pegged furniture joints become part of the total scheme. Accessories, however, play the dominant role in establishing the Colonial mood. Soft pewter dinnerware, woven baskets, wrought iron or wooden antiques are found clustered on the hearth, mounted on walls or hung overhead. A Colonial kitchen, as you will see in the following pages is not stark and sterile but projects the honest comfortable clutter of a real family that works, plays and enjoys life together.

Opposite: The use of textured materials, rough sawn wood ceiling and overhead beams, pecky wall paneling, tile countertop and antique brick on walls and floors, generates a traditional mood for this modern Colonial kitchen. Antique hanging lamps, pewter candlestick and teapot are among the accessories used to evoke an Early American "feel".

Colonial Kitchens Today

17th Century Charm, 20th Century Comfort

No matter how much you appreciate Colonial houses, history and antiques, a restored family room/kitchen must still be functional enough to handle the demands of a working mother with four active children. At the right, photos illustrate how one family in upstate New York was able to marry the original personality of a 1696 Dutch Colonial cottage with materials and appliances of today's home. Salvaged brick and a weathered timber were used to rebuild the family room fireplace. The wrought iron andirons and spark screen reflect the patina of the antique cast iron kettle and skillets surrounding the fireplace. A well-loved maple rocker with comfortable cushion sits on a colorful braided rug before the warm hearth. Below, the kitchen area takes full advantage of the compact 8'x5' floor space. Overhead, a wrought iron lighting fixture and swag of dried herbs hang from the hand-adzed beams. Soft copper-toned refrigerator and range are in perfect color harmony with the mellow wood tones of the birch cabinets and paneling. The "colonial" dishwasher was purchased with an empty frame front and a stained wood panel was added to match the birch cabinetry. The kitchen floor is a rich cinnamon brown vinyl tile, decorative and practical.

Details Can Make the Difference

Below: Through careful attention to materials, hardware and lighting effects, Roberta Griffin, ASID, was able to recreate the charm of a Dutch Colonial kitchen without sacrificing its day-to-day family efficiency. The kitchen area and family room were walled with antique aged brick and the glazed tile splash board over the sink added an authentic and practical touch. Kitchen cabinets were naturally finished and hung with period H and L hinge hardware. The curved timbered beam over the kitchen entrance was constructed with massive wooden trunnels to duplicate 17th Century construction practices. Overhead spotlighting in kitchen ceiling and valance back light behind owners' antique beer stein collection cast a warm, inviting glow over both vintage rooms.

Photography: John Hartley

Photography: Old House Journal

Photography: Armstrong Cork Co. (above), Ethan Allen (below)

Colonial Kitchens

Pewter Accessories Set the Tone

Opposite top: Accessories, both practical and decorative, go a long way toward establishing a warm and inviting Colonial kitchen atmosphere. Pewter dishes, goblets and tankard on the circular wood table reflect a soft glow from the wrought iron chandelier overhead. The plate rail above the pecky cypress wall paneling displays a collection of antique plates with pitchers, mugs and trays showcased in the ornate wood cabinet featuring decoratively turned columns. Below, the antique quilt patterns are repeated in the vinyl flooring and wallpaper designs. The family room incorporates a black cast iron fireplace, comfortable furnishings and one-of-a-kind electrified lantern and old-fashioned sled as mood setting wall decorations. An area rug adds a touch of warmth.

Furniture Choice is Authentic and Mellow

Opposite bottom: This gourmet corner is a good example of how the Early American image can be recreated in today's kitchen without sacrificing the functional needs of an active family. Maple, a traditional hardwood with pleasing grain characteristics, was used throughout. Stained a warm brown, then finished in a durable, low sheen protective coating, the wood provides a perfect foil for copper, brass and pewter accessories. The modular wall unit provides storage areas and display space for a treasured metal and china plate collection. The corner desk, upright shelves and narrow trestle table form a U-shaped work area. Hand stenciled decorations on the bench back and ladder back chair blend with the wallpaper pattern to enhance the Colonial feeling.

Extra Space Through Custom Cabinetry

The Early kitchen, with a few basic cooking utensils and a limited amount of non-perishable foods, managed with a limited amount of storage space. Today, however, the modern kitchen demands generous storage areas that would be the envy of a Colonial housewife. In the kitchen below, white porcelain knobs contrast with the dark stained knotty pine custom cabinets. Along the back wall, several stand up units and cabinets over the sink area hold cleaning supplies and food stuffs. Cooking and serving utensils are housed in the island cabinets handy to the surface range and chopping block built into the top. Additional cabinets over the refrigerator and along the left hand wall and counter provide extra storage for food and table setting hardware.

Photography: General Electric

Colonial Kitchens

Decor Features Antique Collection

Right: Hanging over the stove is a collection of antique cooking utensils — gaily hand-painted ceramic mixing spoons, strainers, mugs and jars. A tole painted tin cake box with bread board and pie cover can be seen on the righthand counter. The stained knotty pine cabinets feature hand wrought handles and H and L hinges. In the foreground, an ancient nail box, crudely fashioned and painted, holds silverware for the table. The circular table itself, has a base made up of an antique coffee grinder. A unique collection blended into a working kitchen.

Textures Make a Country Kitchen

Below: This homespun style of decorating recalls pioneer days when the heart of the home was the "keeping room" where those in the household spent most of their time. It was here that the cooking was done, the meals eaten and members of the family sometimes slept. There is a warm, old-fashioned charm about this kitchen designed by Faye Bodeen of Cannell & Chaffin. The brick fireplace, rough mantel and ceiling beams, tile flooring and back splash over the sink, maple chopping block and round oak dining table provide honest texture in this nostalgic kitchen.

Photography: John Hartley

Compact living on single floor

PLAN 3325

Tall, narrow shutters and the four column porch lend a feeling of height to this single story Colonial charmer. The interior layout has four bedrooms and two baths on the righthand side; at the left is the living room and family room with fireplace, efficient kitchen, handy to both the formal dining room and the breakfast area, with a large utility room and storage space behind the two-auto carport. Mirror reverse plans available if specified at no extra cost; materials list is an additional $10. This easy care home can be built on a slab, crawl space or full basement construction. Please specify foundation.

Designer: W. L. Corley

TO ORDER
BUILDING BLUEPRINTS
USE ORDER FORM
ON PAGE 111

Living Area . . . 1830 sq. ft.

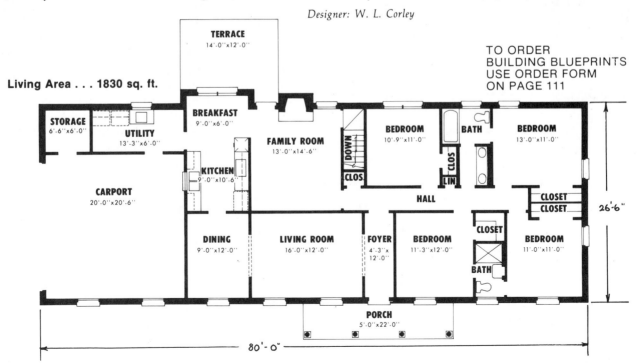

B. NATHAN.

Open ceilings plus expandable options

PLAN 2411

The exterior of this well-proportioned Colonial home features the traditional narrow wood siding and small paned windows associated with early designs. Yet interior surprises include the high ceiling line in both the large entry hall and the family-living room. The U-shaped kitchen faces an oversize fireplace across the room with a nearby laundry and breakfast area. Two large bedrooms and a full bath are on the first floor with two additional bedrooms and another bath planned for the unfinished second story. Mirror reverse plans available if specified at no additional cost.

Designer: William M. Thompson, AIA

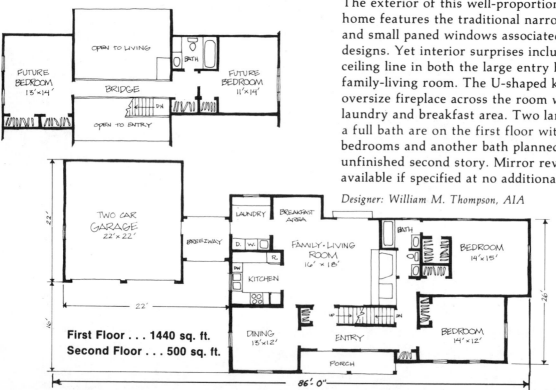

First Floor . . . 1440 sq. ft.
Second Floor . . . 500 sq. ft.

Tri-level with Colonial facade

PLAN 4206

The multi-levels of this rambling house make it possible for a family to involve itself in a variety of different activities, all at the same time. Ground level entry conveniently channels traffic into the large family room beyond or via a short flight of stairs to the upper levels. Compact laundry and a half-bath are well placed off the family room. Upstairs, the living and sleeping quarters are separated by another slight elevation and a hallway. Top level contains master and two smaller-size bedrooms plus a full bath and ample closets. Mirror reverse plans available if specified.

Designer: Claude Miquelle Associates

TO ORDER
BUILDING BLUEPRINTS
USE ORDER FORM
ON PAGE 111

Upper Levels . . . 1138 sq. ft.
Lower Level . . . 300 sq. ft.

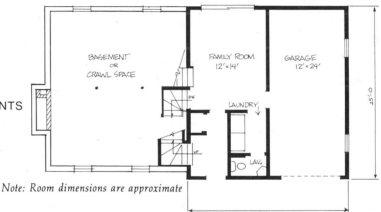

Note: Room dimensions are approximate

B·NATHAN.

Spacious home for larger family

PLAN 2718

If yours is a larger-than-average family, or you frequently entertain guests, you'll appreciate this very spacious dwelling. The plan includes four bedrooms and two full baths on the second level; a single bedroom and full bath on the first floor. The kitchen and adjoining family room with fireplace span the rear of the house with easy access provided from both to an outdoor patio. A materials list is included. Mirror reverse plans are available if specified.

Designer: Henry D. Norris, AIA

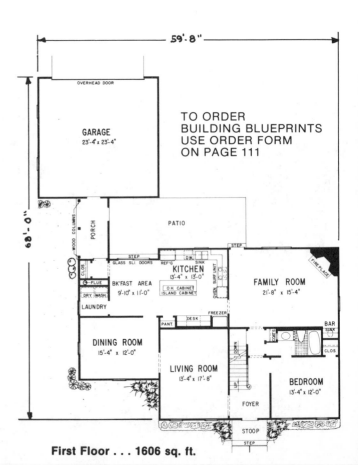

TO ORDER
BUILDING BLUEPRINTS
USE ORDER FORM
ON PAGE 111

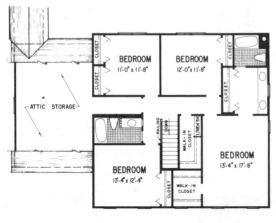

Second Floor . . . 1224 sq. ft.

First Floor . . . 1606 sq. ft.

Bedroom fireplace creates special mood

PLAN 2710

The master bedroom of this home includes a private bath, dressing area with his and her walk-in closets and features a fireplace for those cozy winter evenings. Three additional bedrooms, full bath and huge play-hobby room over the garage complete the second floor. U-shaped kitchen on first floor contains center work island with breakfast area and laundry nearby. Book-lined fireplace in family room backs up to additional fireplace in living room. Materials list is included. Mirror reverse plans are available if specified at no extra cost.

Designer: Henry D. Norris, AIA

First Floor . . . 1885 sq. ft.
Second Floor . . . 1986 sq. ft.

Compact Early American farmhouse

PLAN 5909

The original home on which this plan is based was first built as a farmhouse in Massachusetts. Judged as a fine example of the early gambrel roof style, it has been relocated at Sturbridge Village where it has been preserved for future generations. The basic ground floor plan includes both living room and family room with fireplaces, a study or bedroom with bath and a U-shaped kitchen in the rear. The second story, beneath the double-sloped roof, contains two bedrooms and a bath. Mirror reverse plans are available if specified at no extra cost and materials list is included.

Designer: Evan Pollitt, Architect

First Floor . . . 1046 sq. ft.
Basement . . . 1046 sq. ft.

Suggested GARAGE Location

KITCHEN 15'x9'
refrig
surface units
oven
sink

FAMILY ROOM 15'x12'

PORCH

STUDY OR BED ROOM 10'x11'

books

UP

LIVING ROOM 13'-6" x 18'

DN

closet   shower   coats

42'-6"

34'-6"

BED ROOM 11'-6 x 10   cl.   cl.   closet   BED ROOM 13'-6 x 12'-6

Second Floor . . . 525 sq. ft.

TO ORDER
BUILDING BLUEPRINTS
USE ORDER FORM
ON PAGE 111

Large Colonial
for an expanding family

PLAN 2242

The clean exterior lines of narrow clapboard siding are balanced by the unusually tall shutters beside the windows and raised panel entrance door of this traditional home. The second floor offers a master bedroom, dressing area and private bath with three additional bedrooms and a bath. Space over the garage may be expanded into a studio, hobby area or fifth bedroom. On the first floor, a lavatory, large pantry and mud room off the kitchen are featured. Full reverse plans are available for an additional $30. Materials list is included.

Designer: National Plan Service

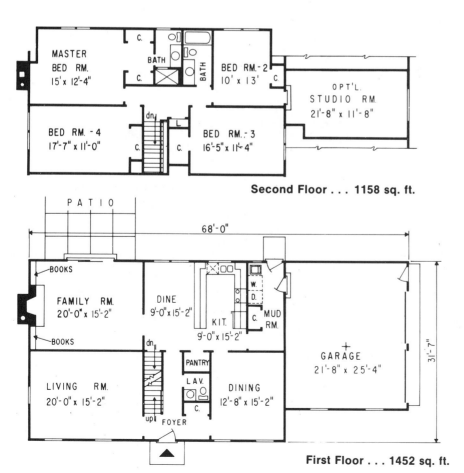

Second Floor . . . 1158 sq. ft.

MASTER BED RM. 15' x 12'-4"

BED RM. - 2 10' x 13'

OPT'L. STUDIO RM. 21'-8" x 11'-8"

BED RM. - 4 17'-7" x 11'-0"

BED RM. - 3 16'-5" x 11'-4"

BATH

PATIO

68'-0"

31'-7"

BOOKS

FAMILY RM. 20'-0" x 15'-2"

DINE 9'-0" x 15'-2"

KIT. 9'-0" x 15'-2"

W. D.

MUD RM.

BOOKS

GARAGE 21'-8" x 25'-4"

LIVING RM. 20'-0" x 15'-2"

PANTRY

LAV.

DINING 12'-8" x 15'-2"

FOYER

First Floor . . . 1452 sq. ft.

B. NATHAN

Stately columns accent Southern hospitality

PLAN 3326

A gracious Southern Colonial design creates a warm welcome as guests pass beneath the two-story front porch supported by six impressive columns. The foyer features a curved staircase which sweeps to the upstairs bedrooms and baths. Spacious rooms on the ground level include large kitchen and breakfast area, formal dining room, living room and family room with fireplace. Please specify: slab, crawl space or full basement foundation. Mirror reverse plans available if specified at no additional cost; materials list costs an extra $10.

Designer: W. L. Corley

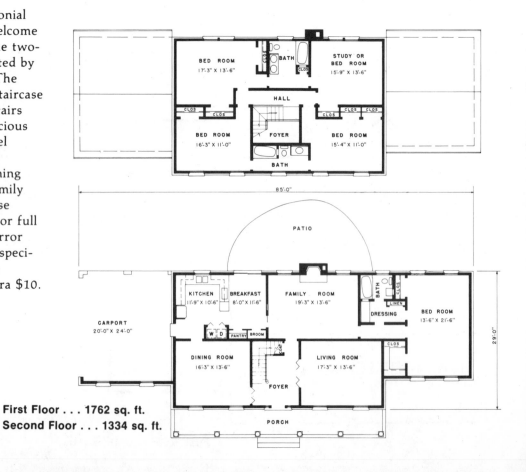

First Floor . . . 1762 sq. ft.
Second Floor . . . 1334 sq. ft.

Clustered work area opens living space

Second Floor . . . 1040 sq. ft.

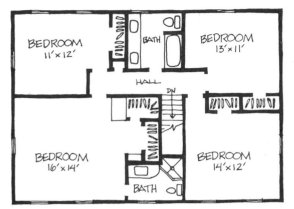

BEDROOM 11'×12'
BATH
BEDROOM 13'×11'
HALL
DN
BEDROOM 16'×14'
BEDROOM 14'×12'
BATH

PLAN 2412

A carefully designed floor plan isolates the kitchen, breakfast area, laundry and lavatory in the rear of this two-story early Colonial home. This provides space for a large front-to-rear living room with fireplace, formal dining room and large family room with fireplace on the garage wall. The second floor features four bedrooms, two baths and generous closet space. The traditionally designed exterior is highlighted by the overhanging second story facade. Mirror reverse plans available if specified at no additional cost. Materials list is included.

Designer: William M. Thompson, AIA

First Floor . . . 1280 sq. ft.

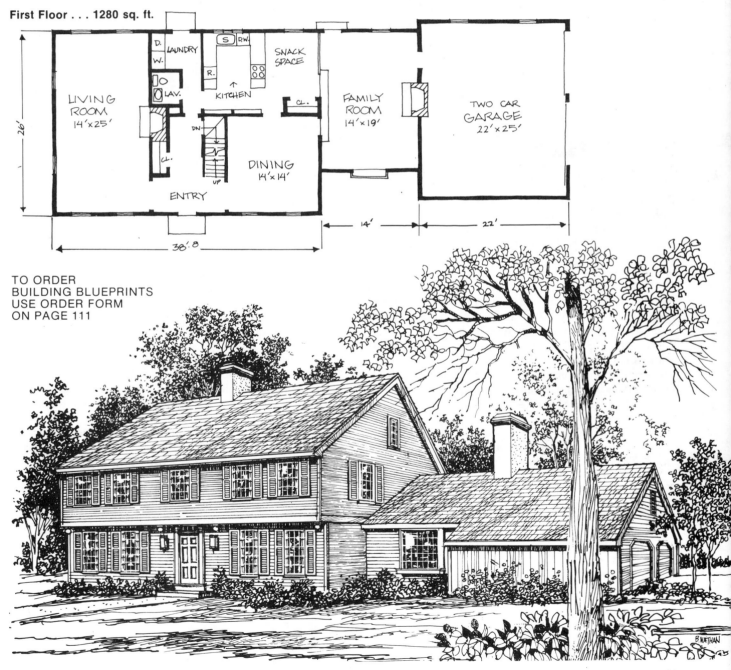

D.
LAUNDRY
S
D.W.
SNACK SPACE
W.
R.
LIVING ROOM 14'×25'
LAV.
KITCHEN
CL.
FAMILY ROOM 14'×19'
TWO CAR GARAGE 22'×25'
26'
DN.
CL.
DINING 14'×14'
UP
ENTRY
CL.
14'
22'
38'.8

TO ORDER
BUILDING BLUEPRINTS
USE ORDER FORM
ON PAGE 111

B NATHAN

Photography: Ethan Allen

Dining in the Traditional Manner

Eating can be the basic process of restoking the human body with energy producing foods to carry on additional hours of labor. Dining, however, represents a time shared with family and friends that rises above the strictly functional intake of calories. Dining, whether casual or formal, should be as relaxed and enjoyable for the host as for his guests. Early American fare was usually produced from the family garden, raised in the barnyard or shot in the nearby woods, and then baked in the oven built into the fireplace. Today, the world is your bread basket. With efficient transportation and improvements in processing and preservation techniques, food and drink is collected from fields, orchards and vineyards in dozens of countries. Tropical fruits may grace a mid-winter table, ethnic foods and pastries produce an instant geography lesson while a wine tasting party can expose a series of domestic and foreign taste sensations. There never has been a more exciting time to sit down at the table. Sometimes the food is the star of the show but often, dining area decor, the table setting or the warm conversation of close friends upstages the food. Colonial furnishings were usually of native woods, pine, birch, maple, oak and later mahogany, stained and polished to a dull sheen reflecting the soft glow from overhead lighting, wall sconces or table candles. The styling varied since the design period spanned everything from the simple, primitive handmade lines of earliest Pilgrim New England to the stately and classic forms of the tidewater Southern colonies represented by talented native craftsmen/ designers such as Duncan Phyfe and other American cabinetmakers. Illustrated on the following pages are Colonial dining rooms using the traditional designs as reproduced today by contemporary manufacturers. The opportunity exists to blend the styling, materials, muted colors and bold patterns of Colonial decorating into a personal statement expressing your hospitality.

A modern Colonial dining room projects a feeling of warmth and grace. Dark finished pine trestle benches and table and hand stenciled ladder back chairs with woven rush seats invite guests to enjoy an informal coffee and dessert.

Traditional Dining

Shell Carvings on Queen Anne Design

The classic curves of Queen Anne styling are evident in the sweep of the back, arm and leg of table and chairs in this tasteful dining scene. An added accent is the shell carved motif found on the upper table leg and chair back. Across the room, the china cabinet features a carved broken pediment top with subtle dentil moulding applied beneath. The curved theme is repeated in the deep window valances with their scalloped edges and the flow of the brass chandelier over the dining table. The table setting is simple and elegant. Around the floral centerpiece, the place settings are dominated by the tall glassware. From the fragments found at Colonial Williamsburg, these reproductions are made of lead glass, strong yet translucent, and hand-formed one at a time by experienced craftsmen. The traditional wallpaper employs a colorful floral pattern. At the floor level are stained and highly polished random oak planks.

Good Design is Versatile

Illustrated below, a second Queen Anne styled dining room shows the versatility within a period design. This manufacturer relied more on the natural wood grain combined with the pure design form to accent the 18th century lines. The buffet with china display top on the rear walls has the authentic Queen Anne arch motif on the paneled doors which is repeated for the doors in the top. Details include grooved top shelves, dentil moulding, scalloped edges and classic ogee shaped feet. Brass pulls and hardware are American in design. Three 10-inch filler leaves may be inserted in the formal oval dining table to accommodate additional guests. Two Queen Anne-style armchairs are placed at the table with additional side chairs along the walls. Handsome inlaid parquet wood floor has a mosaic design quality, and the large oriental rug serves to define the dining area in this tastefully appointed late Colonial setting.

Photography: Drexel (opposite), Pennsylvania House (below)

Traditional Dining

Gracious Dining for Two . . . or More

At the right, two photos demonstrate the versatility of Colonial dining rooms to handle an intimate late evening supper or a larger social affair. The oval pedestal supper table, created from glowing Honduras mahogany, is set with antique bone china, sparkling crystal and a handsome silver service. The velvet comfort of the graceful Queen Anne armchairs encourages a leisurely meal in an unhurried atmosphere. Mahogany chests and a turned plant stand maintain the authentic period styling of the room. Floral patterned wallpaper and the rich hues of the oriental rug offer a perfect backdrop to showcase the satin finished wood furnishings. Yet this petite table has two 18-inch leaves to expand the table's top to ninety inches in length for more ambitious entertaining. The larger table below is circled with upholstered chairs with pierced interlaced and carved splats of American Chippendale styling. A richly grained mahogany breakfront with satinwood inlay borders on the base doors and drawers, is top illuminated to showcase the antique china collection. The subtle millwork detailing of the fireplace mantel, brass andirons and hand-painted ceramic tiles surrounding the hearth opening, all add to the well-designed and pleasingly proportioned lines of a traditional Colonial dining room.

An Elegant Setting Based on English Design

The formal dining room illustrated below represents the influence of the English designers Sheraton and Hepplewhite on the 18th century American cabinet-makers. The double pedestal mahogany table features legs with applied brass terminals. The rich grained mahogany top is bordered in lighter satinwood in the Sheraton manner. The dining chairs with pierced interlaced splats and sheaf of wheat carvings are outstanding examples of American chair making based on Thomas Hepplewhite lines. Brass pulls and escutcheons accent the mahogany sideboard, styled after one discovered earlier in Hartford, Connecticut.

Photography: Baker Furniture

Photography: Hickory Furniture

Photography: Cochrane Furniture (top), Pennsylvania House (bottom)

Traditional Dining

Oak and Maple — Traditionally American

The dining rooms shown on the left page illustrate native American woods used to reproduce early Colonial settings. In the top photo, light finished oak allows the sturdy grain to enhance the traditional designs. The double turned base on the round table before the corner fireplace is complemented by the heavily turned construction of the armchair and two side chairs. The dining area is defined by the colorful oval braided rug typical of early keeping rooms. On the brick patterned floor is a similarly styled rocking chair. The oak buffet combines top and center drawers with storage cabinets on either side, and a china top to display ceramic and metal antiques. Below, the maple cross-based dining table was inspired by the "sawbuck" or "X-framed" styles which came to America from England during the late 17th century. The deeply dished chair seats, curved splats and back, are both comfortable to sit in and pleasing to the eye. The well-proportioned buffet, fashioned out of traditional maple, offers a lighted hutch top.

Mahogany Used in Several Styles

The authentic copies of Sheraton, Chippendale and Queen Anne designs shown below, have been scaled down to better adapt to today's smaller rooms. While retaining their classic lines and proportions, each mahogany piece has been scaled to fit comfortably into a modern Colonial dining room. For all its traditional American styling, the setting takes on a decidedly Oriental flavor through blending of the wallpaper, subtle patterns in the rug and dinner plates and the lines of the Chippendale decorative chair backs. Thomas Chippendale, the English cabinetmaker, borrowed elements from Gothic, Chinese and French designs and translated them into a fresh style. While native American woods were usually employed in Colonial furniture, any skilled craftsman preferred to work with the tight, close-grained mahogany when creating the crisp carvings associated with Chippendale designs. The early woodworkers took full advantage of various wood characteristics and often mixed several species in the same piece of furniture.

Photography: Drexel

New materials recreate Colonial details

PLAN 2723

The Early American builder fashioned the many decorative mouldings and detailed millwork patterns with simple hand tools. Today, many of these traditional profiles are readily available. This two-story exterior facade recreates the classic detailing. The floor plan offers a large kitchen and breakfast area, formal dining room, lavatory, study and family room with fireplace on the first level. Four bedrooms and two baths complete the second floor. Mirror reverse plans available if specified and a materials list is included with plans.

Designer: Henry D. Norris, AIA

First Floor . . . 1439 sq. ft.
Second Floor . . . 1240 sq. ft.

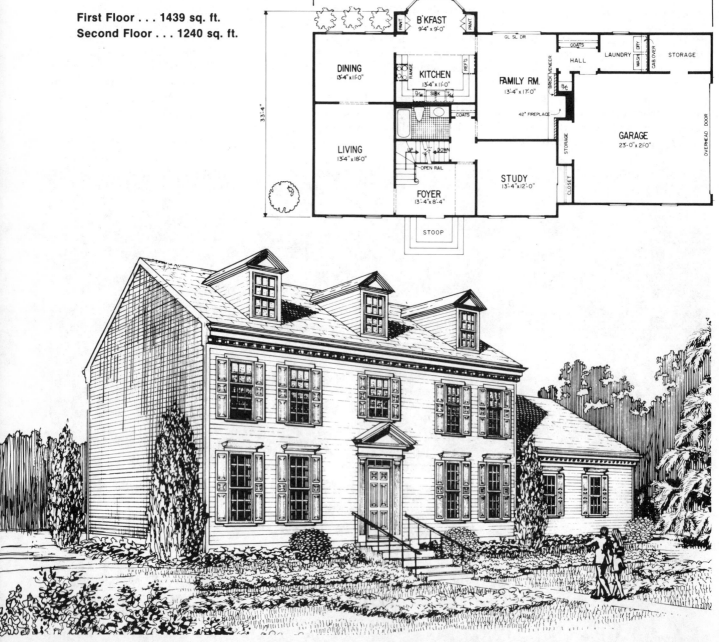

Kitchen enjoys diamond window view

PLAN 4209

By placing the kitchen in the front of the home, the architect of this home allowed the housewife to enjoy the traditional small diamond-shaped window panes associated with Colonial styling. Other rooms on the first level include a dining room, living room with fireplace and two large bedrooms plus a bath. The second story features three large and unusually shaped bedrooms and a full bath. The double car garage, offset at an angle, is attached to the house by a covered porch. Horizontal exterior lines are broken by the chimney and garage cupolas. If specified, mirror reverse plans are available at no extra cost.

Designer: Claude Miquelle Associates

TO ORDER
BUILDING BLUEPRINTS
USE ORDER FORM
ON PAGE 111

Second Floor . . . 880 sq. ft.

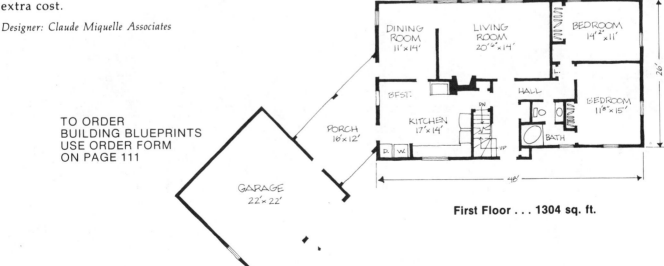

First Floor . . . 1304 sq. ft.

A floor plan zoned for privacy

PLAN 3321

This palatial Southern Colonial mansion has 2800 square feet of living area, well-organized into living zones. The master bedroom has its own private wing, including two walk-in closets and a full bath. L-shaped kitchen, dining room and breakfast area are all adjacent for convenience. Large family room has a woodburning fireplace and is located in the rear of the home, while formal living room has direct access from the entry hall. Materials list costs an extra $10; mirror reverse plans available if specified. Please specify which foundation: slab, crawl space or full basement.

Designer: W. L. Corley

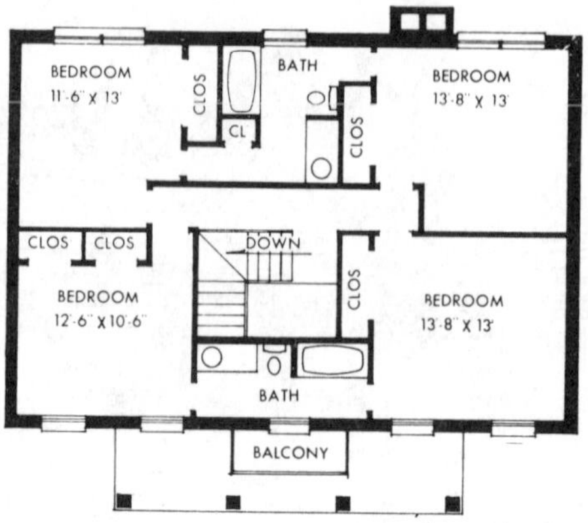

Second Floor . . . 1148 sq. ft.

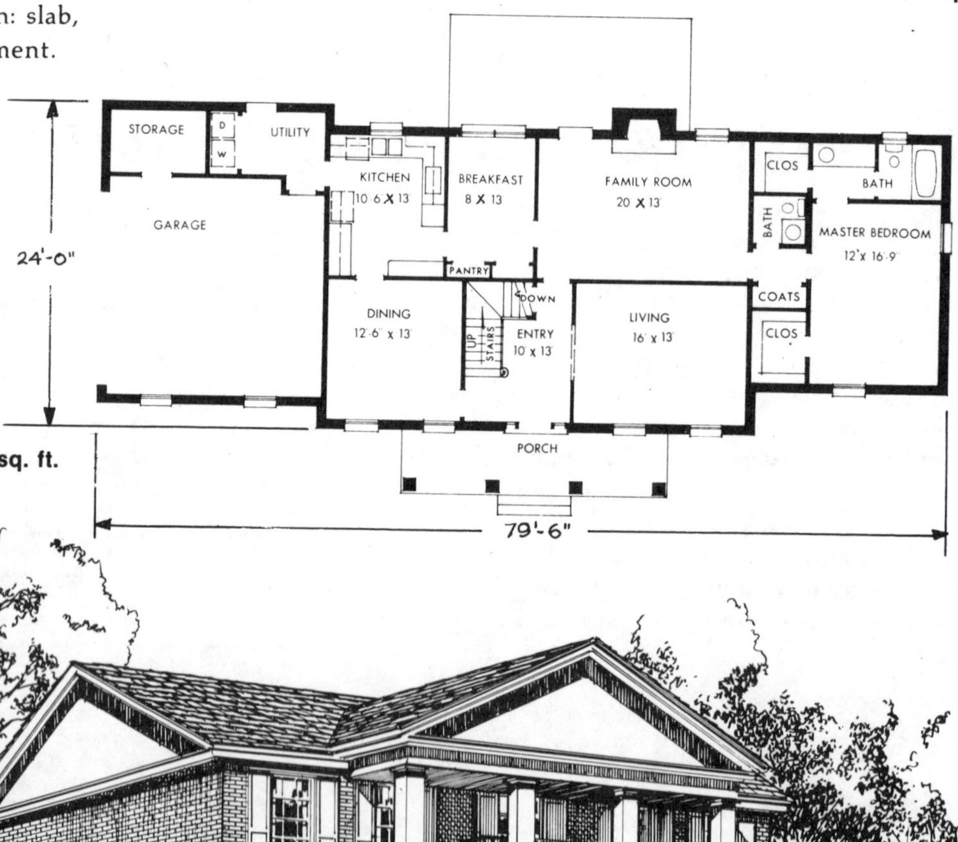

First Floor . . . 1652 sq. ft.

Simple design projects Colonial charm

PLAN 2243

The strong traditional design of the home shown here relies on balanced styling rather than fussy detail. Clipped corners on garage doors create a hint of the era of covered bridges and horse drawn wagons. Inside, the foyer with its open stairway and balustrades leads to four bedrooms and two baths on the second floor. The main floor features a family room with beamed ceiling and natural fireplace. Central hall provides easy access to living room, large kitchen, powder room, laundry and garage. Materials list is included; full reverse plans are available for $30 extra.

Designer: National Plan Service

TO ORDER
BUILDING BLUEPRINTS
USE ORDER FORM
ON PAGE 111

First Floor . . . 1106 sq. ft.
Second Floor . . . 1092 sq. ft.

75

Colonial ranch is long and low

PLAN 5910

Combining traditional styling and modern efficiency, this Colonial ranch home has a large living room with a bay window and fireplace, while the family room has its own fireplace and large window in the front. The easily maintained one floor plan includes three bedrooms, lots of closet space and two baths. Separate laundry, closet and lavatory are grouped near the garage entry with access from front and rear. Covered porch between house and garage provides sheltered area. Materials list is included. If specified, mirror reverse plans are available at no additional cost.

Designer: Evan Pollitt, Architect

Living Area . . . 2100 sq. ft.
Basement . . . 2100 sq. ft.

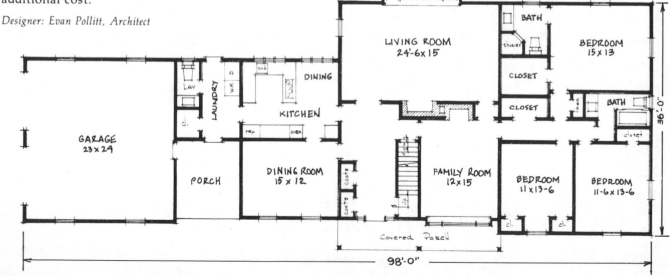

First floor is open, second is private

PLAN 2244

This two-story Colonial with overhanging upper level, captures the best of both worlds. The large L-shaped kitchen and breakfast area opens onto the family room for full enjoyment of the fireplace. Formal dining room, living room and lavatory off the entry complete the first floor. Upstairs are two bedrooms and a bath plus the master bedroom suite with private bath, walk-in closet and special bonus parents' hide-away room for those quiet moments. Full reverse plans are available for $30 additional; complete materials list is included.

Designer: National Plan Service

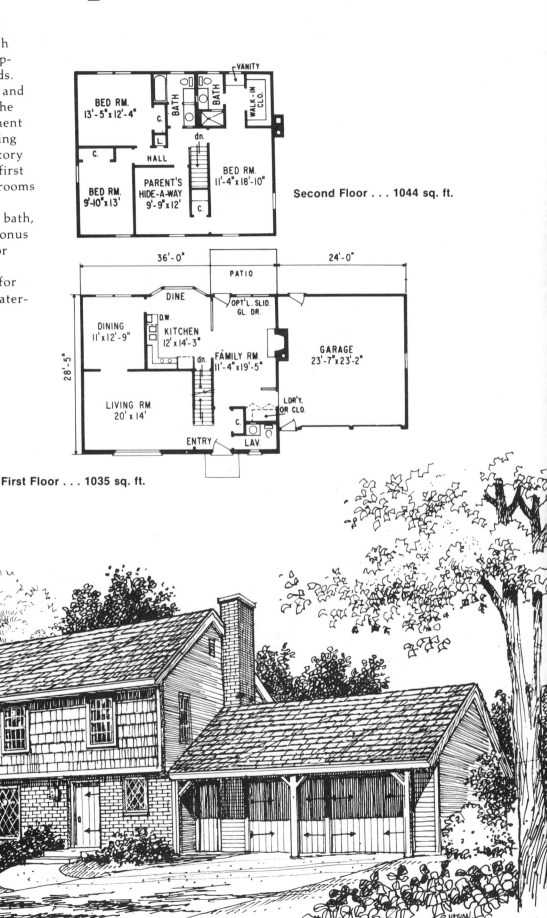

Second Floor ... 1044 sq. ft.

First Floor ... 1035 sq. ft.

B. NATHAN

Bricks and columns create Southern Colonial

PLAN 2245

A two-story Southern Colonial uses brick siding and four tall columns to establish a cool and comfortable atmosphere. The gracious entry is through a raised panel entrance door flanked with sidelights. A large living room faces the front with dining room, kitchen and breakfast area in the rear. The family room with fireplace has access to the patio. The second floor is made up of four bedrooms and two baths, plus another large room which may be used as a study. Materials list is included; full reverse plans are available for an additional $30.

Designer: National Plan Service

First Floor . . . 1258 sq. ft.

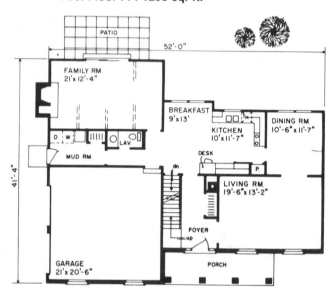

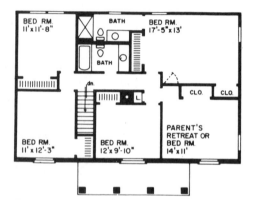

Second Floor . . . 1176 sq. ft.

Large Cape Cod cottage loaded with extras

Second Floor . . . 1135 sq. ft.

Second Floor labels:
- BEDROOM 16'-0" x 13'-0"
- CLOSET
- BATH
- BATH
- LIN
- WALK-IN CLOSET
- CLOS
- BEDROOM 11'-0" x 12'-7"
- HALL
- BEDROOM 14'-0" x 16'-7"
- CLOS
- STOR
- CLOS
- STORAGE ROOM
- folding stairs
- dwn

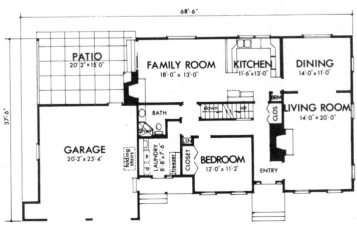

First Floor . . . 1383 sq. ft.

First Floor labels:
- 68'-6"
- 37'-6"
- PATIO 20'-2" x 15'-0"
- FAMILY ROOM 18'-0" x 13'-0"
- KITCHEN 11'-6" x 13'-0"
- DINING 14'-0" x 11'-0"
- BATH
- Shwr
- dwn
- up
- BRM
- CLOS
- LIVING ROOM 14'-0" x 20'-0"
- GARAGE 20'-2" x 23'-4"
- folding stairs
- LAUNDRY 8'-8" x 7'-6"
- freezer
- LIN
- CLOSET
- BEDROOM 12'-0" x 11'-2"
- ENTRY

PLAN 3864
PLAN 3864-A (without basement)

Three fireplaces, in the formal living room, family room and upstairs master bedroom suite, make this spacious Cape Cod home a winner. The family room fireplace also doubles as an outside barbecue on the patio. A decorative roof dormer lets extra light into the front bedroom and a large rear bedroom has double closets. A downstairs bedroom off the entry hall offers accommodations for guests or as an extra room for crafts, den or study. Extra storage is provided over the double-car garage. Materials list costs an additional $20; full reverse plans are available for an extra $20.

Designer: Home Building Plan Service

TO ORDER
BUILDING BLUEPRINTS
USE ORDER FORM
ON PAGE 111

Photography: American Drew, Inc.

Bedrooms with a Period Look

"Early to bed and early to rise . . .", the old Colonial maxim was a harsh reality for the original settlers. Survival meant long hours of hard labor and sleeping quarters were often a corner of the keeping room not too far from the warmth of the hearth. But as both the new nation and its citizens prospered, homes became larger and the separate bedroom was established. The beds to which the early colonists retired were usually primitive wooden frames laced with rope "springs" or built-in units styled more like a ship's bunk, often with a pull out trundle bed beneath for the children. The more affluent opted for tester beds which dated back to medieval times. The four corner posts of the testers were draped in heavy fabric that provided some measure of privacy and protection from the ever present drafts of earliest homes. Elaborately carved and turned tester beds were imported from France and England, but in time, American craftsmen reproduced the item borrowing and modifying the European designs. The style remains popular today and on the following pages are shown various four poster and tester beds used in traditional surroundings. Today's multi-purpose bedroom provides space for sleeping, catching up on correspondence and simply a quiet spot to enjoy a moment of privacy. Since it represents one of the most intimate areas of the home, the bedroom should reflect your personal interests and color preferences. It's your space, so make it as frilly or functional as you desire. In allocating space, begin your planning with the bed. It's the largest piece of furniture in the room so position it first and design around it. Storage facilities come next. Perhaps a large dresser with mirror and an armoire or highboy. Then several comfortable chairs, perhaps one a rocker, and a small table or writing desk. Consider a low bench or antique blanket chest for the foot of the bed. Now the furnishings can be accented and blended into a total scheme through use of accessories, personal items and the choice of wallpaper, drapes, rugs and bedspread patterns which may complement or match each other. The Colonial period offers a variety of fabric and furniture styles to create from. Blend the classic antiques and the modern-day antique reproductions into your own personal statement and decorative scheme.

The Colonial bedroom shown at the right uses a bold floral pattern in the wallpaper which is repeated in the drapes and bedspread. Four poster bed has a broken pediment headboard echoed in the mirror and handsome twelve drawer maple highboy.

Bedrooms

Maple and Pine — Native American Grains

Traditional maple and pine furnishings in the bedroom setting on the top of the opposite page, allow the strong American native grains to dominate the scheme. Curly maple veneer, with its distinctive patterns, was a sound choice for the compact Colonial bedroom tucked beneath a beamed sloped roof. Cannonball bed, unique hutch mirror dresser and chest on chest storage unit give a feeling of solid warmth to the room. Random-width pegged plank flooring with an oval braided rug add informality. Fabric used on the bedspread dust ruffles matches the colorfully striped wallpaper pattern. In the photo below, Early American pine and simple styling create a modern Colonial bedroom. The bed and two small night tables are recessed into a shallow alcove with arched top. The white rough-plastered wall frames the rustic barn-siding wood wall treatment behind the bed. At the left behind the pine dresser and mirror, the barnsiding has been applied in a diagonal fashion to lead the eye toward the revolutionary ancestor portrait over the headboard. Touches of color are provided by the homespun striped spread and an oval hooked rug on the painted plank flooring. The use of a few key accessories points out the effectiveness of a few simple items in recreating a traditional Colonial bedroom.

French-Canadian Artistry and Design

Unusual French-Colonial styling developed in the northern settlements along the Canadian border. Below, a charming bedroom setting reproduced in pickled ash wood captures the light natural-toned wood highlights to balance pastel blue color of the bedside lamp base. The carved sweep of the headboard and deeply fluted posts is repeated in the dresser and mirror, small tables and large freestanding armoire. Neutral grass cloth wallcovering provides a backdrop to accent furnishings. Rush-bottom chair in the foreground sits on deep pile carpet which matches the restful blue of the bedspread.

Photography: The Stiffel Co. (below); Stanley Furniture (opposite page)

Photography: John Hartley (above); Pulaski Furniture Co. (below)

Simplicity is the Key to Colonial Design

Strength in simplicity is often the hallmark of pleasing Colonial interiors. With all the fascinating antiques — fireplace tools, dinnerware, lamps and sconces — the temptation is to over accessorize an Early American setting. Fight the temptation. As the two photos on the adjoining page prove, a simple, uncluttered interior scheme often becomes more effective. The top photo illustrates a bedroom feature you will find in several home floor plans within this book. The ground level bedroom, isolated from the general traffic flow, enjoys a private deck or patio. When you add the bonus of a fireplace, the large bedroom becomes a retreat for the parents. Here, comfort is paramount with two Victorian needlepoint upholstered chairs by the small writing table and a pair of overstuffed chairs with a good reading lamp before the cheerful hearth. The cushioned stools at the foot of the beds serve as extra seating or to support folded bedspreads. Below, a small bedroom is dominated by the spindle-top high-poster bed of deep grained golden oak. Bentwood captain's chair features spindle back with cane woven top. The three-panel folding screen on paw's feet roll-away casters matches the steamer trunk with leather straps and shiny brass hardware.

Photography: Ege Rya, Inc. (below)

Traditional Bedroom that Combines Periods

Pattern on pattern treatment used in the bedroom below is a difficult to handle but highly rewarding design ploy. The Early American stencil-patterned wallpaper has a reverse color design used in the bed tester canopy and bedspread. The geometric pattern bordering the mirror over the mantel is repeated in the window alcove area. Additional period design elements within the bed-sitting room are found in the Art Nouveau pattern floor rug, tea service on the butler's tray and needlepoint cushion in the tub chair before the fireplace. The varying designs are held together by use of a monochromatic color scheme: blue and white.

Bedrooms

Light Fixtures Can Set the Mood

Proper lighting sets the mood in any room, but its importance is sometimes overlooked when designing the sleeping areas. The light level or levels depends upon when and how the bedroom is used. If it functions primarily as a sleep center, subdued illumination with perhaps a good bedside reading lamp, may be all that is necessary. If, however, the room serves several purposes at different times of the day, then extra care will assure the right level of light for study, sewing or hobby activities or pleasant conversation. At the left, a lamp on the dresser lights the mirror, bedside table lamp is used for evening reading and the overhead brass and crystal chandelier provides general illumination and a classic aura for the entire room. Matching prints are seen on the draperies, bed dust ruffles and pillows against the headboard. Below, a pair of brass coach lamp reproductions flank the bed. On the dresser, a handsome reproduction of a brass whale oil lamp, often favored by Nantucket ship captains, lights the mirror. Hardwood candle sconces on the far wall are more decorative than functional. Natural sunlight, streaming through the French doors, provides a delightful incentive to greet the new day each morning. Pine wood trunk adds a decorative and informal feel, as does the multi-colored, braided oval rug.

Photography: Idaka (above), Kimball Furniture (below)

Bicentennial Renews Colonial Interest

Thanks to the recent Bicentennial celebration during 1976, the American public and, more importantly, American manufacturers have begun to appreciate the rich heritage derived from the Colonial period. What started as crude survival evolved and matured into a variety of highly refined styles, tastes and techniques. The structural and decorative aspects of native and imported woods, cast metal work, hammered and spun into practical and pleasing shapes, the interplay of colors and patterns in wallcoverings, fabrics and ceramics all have re-awakened an interest in Early American lifestyles. Many of the manufacturers listed in our index have established or broadened their lines to make it easier than ever for today's homemaker to decorate rooms with quality and authentic reproductions. For instance, the wallpaper and fabric industries, as shown at the right, have combined talents to provide matching materials. This design is adapted from the famous "Tree of Life" pattern brought back by clipper ship captains sailing the exotic Indian Ocean during the early 1800's. Below, the art of hand stenciling is being revived with special patterns, paints and brushes now available to recreate the charming effect. This scene uses stencils at the ceiling line, on the beams and to frame the window alcove.

Photography: Wallcovering Industry Bureau (above), Drexel Furniture (below)

Connecticut salt box with add-ons

PLAN 5911

This early New England salt box possesses authentic proportions and lines. The laundry and garage have been added on in the Colonial manner for modern convenience. The floor plan presents an L-shaped kitchen and dining area, large family or keeping room with corner fireplace and a living room with fireplace. First floor level includes a master bedroom with walk-in closet and private bath. Two bedrooms and bath on second floor may be finished as needed. Materials list included; mirror reverse plans available if specified at no extra cost.

Designer: Evan Pollitt, Architect

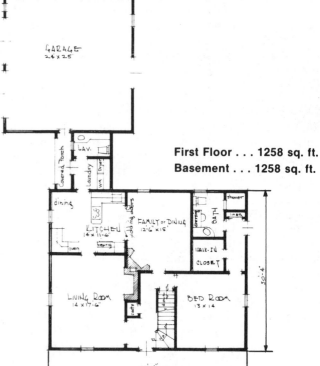

First Floor . . . 1258 sq. ft.
Basement . . . 1258 sq. ft.

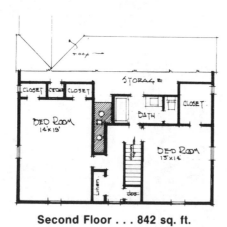

Second Floor . . . 842 sq. ft.

Ideal small family or retirement home

PLAN 2246

Comfortable and snug, this compact Colonial home provides for all the needs of a young couple or retired family in an economical and easy-to-care-for 1531 square feet. The living room-dining area features a large central fireplace and the L-shaped kitchen has a handy breakfast space for snacking. First floor bedroom with adequate closet space has a private bath. The second level contains two large bedrooms and a full bath. Optional plan for two car garage is included. Materials list is included, and full reverse plans are available for an additional $30.

Designer: National Plan Service

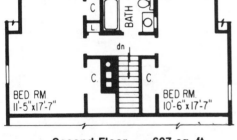

Second Floor . . . 607 sq. ft.

First Floor . . . 924 sq. ft.

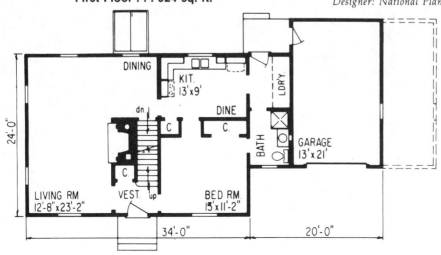

TO ORDER
BUILDING BLUEPRINTS
USE ORDER FORM
ON PAGE 111

Originally a converted barn

PLAN 2413

If you've always dreamed of finding an aged barn to convert, here is your chance. The original conversion was so successful that plans are now available. The huge central chimney contains three fireplaces, one for the living room, a second in the dining room and the largest for a floor-to-ceiling family room in the rear. First floor contains a lavatory and large separate library or den. Rear stairs lead to three unusually large bedrooms and two baths on the second level. Mirror reverse plans available if specified at no additional cost.

Designer: William M. Thompson, AIA

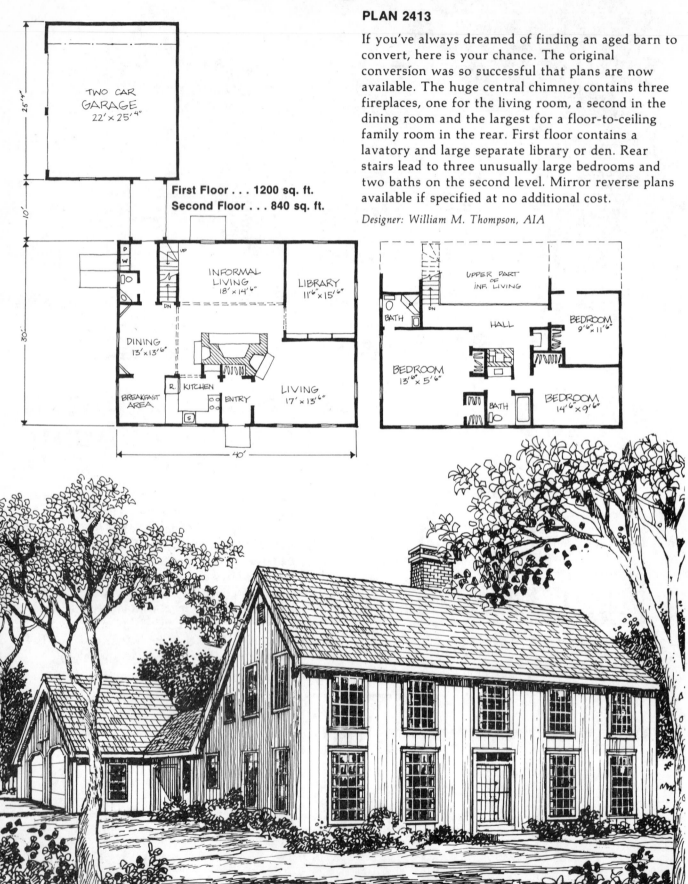

TWO CAR GARAGE
22' x 25'4"

First Floor . . . 1200 sq. ft.
Second Floor . . . 840 sq. ft.

INFORMAL LIVING
18' x 14'6"

LIBRARY
11'6" x 15'6"

DINING
13' x 13'6"

BREAKFAST AREA

KITCHEN

ENTRY

LIVING
17' x 13'6"

BATH

UPPER PART OF INF. LIVING

HALL

BEDROOM
9'6" x 11'6"

BEDROOM
13'6" x 5'6"

BATH

BEDROOM
14'6" x 9'6"

B. NATHAN.

Double sloped roof provides front porch

PLAN 4319

The large front porch of this two-story rustic board-and-batten home creates a warm welcome for arriving guests. To the right of the foyer, a generous-sized activity room with fireplace is separated from the hall by a half wall with Colonial turned spindles above. The country kitchen lays out appliances in an efficient L-shaped plan. Two bedrooms, dressing areas and a full bath are on the first level, with two bedrooms and a bath on the second floor. Mirror reverse plans available if specified; materials list is an additional $10.

Designer: W. D. Farmer

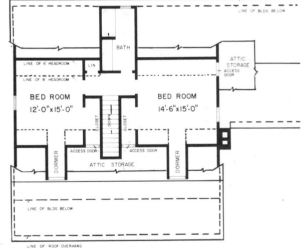

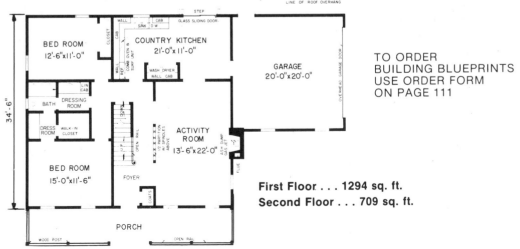

TO ORDER
BUILDING BLUEPRINTS
USE ORDER FORM
ON PAGE 111

First Floor . . . 1294 sq. ft.
Second Floor . . . 709 sq. ft.

Gambrel style provides maximum space

PLAN 2724

Dutch Colonial homes, with gambrel-styled rooflines, take full advantage of second story head room. Here, two full baths and four large bedrooms make up the second floor. The ground level has a formal dining room and living room on either side of the foyer, and across the rear is a large family room with fireplace, breakfast area off the kitchen and a lavatory and laundry. The exterior combines large shuttered windows, brick and wood sidings. Materials list is included, and mirror reverse plans are available if specified at no additional cost.

Designer: Henry D. Norris, AIA

Second Floor . . . 1120 sq. ft.

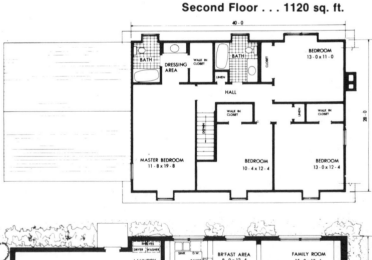

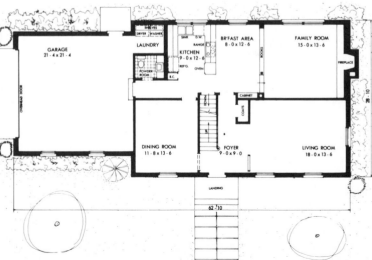

TO ORDER
BUILDING BLUEPRINTS
USE ORDER FORM
ON PAGE 111

First Floor . . . 1234 sq. ft.

Lines from the past ...space for today

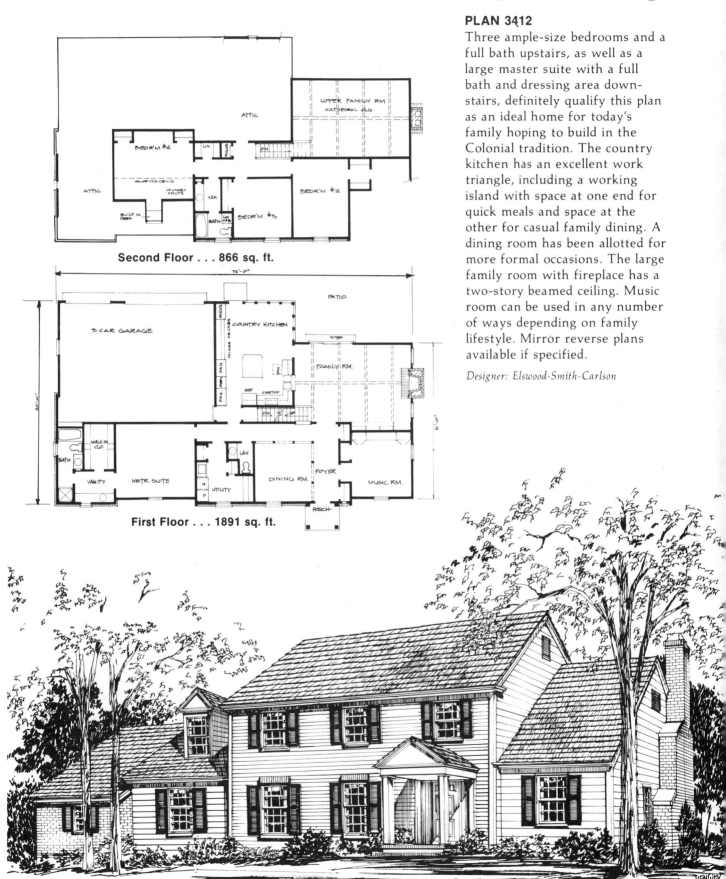

Second Floor . . . 866 sq. ft.

First Floor . . . 1891 sq. ft.

PLAN 3412

Three ample-size bedrooms and a full bath upstairs, as well as a large master suite with a full bath and dressing area downstairs, definitely qualify this plan as an ideal home for today's family hoping to build in the Colonial tradition. The country kitchen has an excellent work triangle, including a working island with space at one end for quick meals and space at the other for casual family dining. A dining room has been allotted for more formal occasions. The large family room with fireplace has a two-story beamed ceiling. Music room can be used in any number of ways depending on family lifestyle. Mirror reverse plans available if specified.

Designer: Elswood-Smith-Carlson

Two-story home with traditional sidings

PLAN 4210

The use of two traditional forms of wood siding, clapboard on the main structure and board and batten on the garage section, reinforce the appearance this structure gives of a Colonial home that grew with the generations. The floor plan provides a living room, dining room, L-shaped kitchen, lavatory and family room with fireplace on the first floor. Four bedrooms and two baths occupy the second floor. The two-car garage, placed at an angle, emphasizes the add-on appeal of early construction. Mirror reverse plans available if specified at no extra cost.

Designer: Claude Miquelle Associates

First Floor . . . 1008 sq. ft.
Second Floor . . . 1008 sq. ft.

TO ORDER
BUILDING BLUEPRINTS
USE ORDER FORM
ON PAGE 111

Large Colonial with hospitable portico

First Floor . . . 2214 sq. ft.
Second Floor . . . 1403 sq. ft.

PLAN 3327

The portico, although not essential in these days of air conditioning, adds to the warm welcoming effect of this brick Southern Colonial home. The foyer stairway leads to two baths and four bedrooms on the second level. The right hand wing contains a master bedroom with walk-in closet, dressing area and full bath. Dining room and living room are in the front with U-shaped kitchen between the utility and breakfast areas. Large den or family room at the rear has book-lined fireplace wall. Please specify foundation when ordering: slab, crawl space or full basement. Mirror reverse plans available if specified; materials list costs an extra $10.

Designer: W. L. Corley

Many Colonial details in one home

PLAN 5912

This gambrel roofed New England home with large central chimney features narrow dormers, twelve over twelve light windows and diamond light windows. The narrow exposure of the clapboards and vertical garage siding suggests an add-on look. Inside, a small book-lined archway links the dining room to the living room with its centered fireplace. A den or bedroom with bath downstairs and three bedrooms plus bath on the second level provide adequate sleeping facilities. Mirror reverse plans are available if specified at no additional cost, and materials list is included.

Designer: Evan Pollitt, Architect

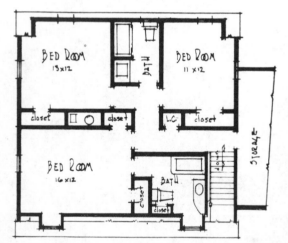

First Floor . . . 1248 sq. ft.
Second Floor . . . 864 sq. ft.
Basement . . . 1248 sq. ft.

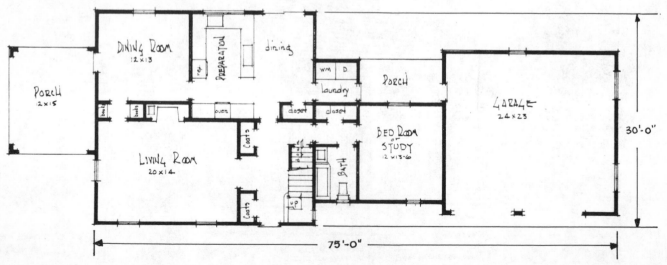

Stone siding creates farmhouse look

PLAN 2725

The rough fieldstone facade of this home recalls the shape and feeling of an Early American farmhouse, yet the look is softened by the large multi-paned windows and the two coach lamps illuminating the paneled entrance door. The traditional detailing is carried inside where the family room with fireplace is separated from the breakfast area by a half wall with turned spindles above. First floor includes master bedroom and bath, with three bedrooms, two baths and a study area on the second floor. Mirror reverse plans available if specified at no extra cost, and complete materials list is included.

Designer: Henry D. Norris, AIA

Second Floor . . . 1100 sq. ft.

First Floor . . . 1508 sq. ft.

TO ORDER
BUILDING BLUEPRINTS
USE ORDER FORM
ON PAGE 111

Classic Colonial offers room to grow

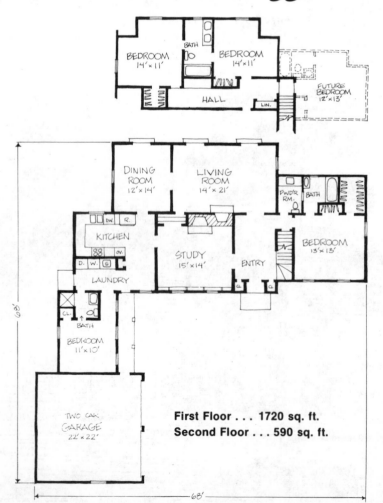

BEDROOM 14'×11'

BATH

BEDROOM 14'×11'

HALL

FUTURE BEDROOM 12'×13'

LIN.

DINING ROOM 12'×14'

LIVING ROOM 14'×21'

PWD'R RM.

BATH

KITCHEN

DW. R.

D.W.

STUDY 15'×14'

ENTRY

BEDROOM 13'×13'

LAUNDRY

CL.

BATH

BEDROOM 11'×13'

TWO CAR GARAGE 22'×22'

68'

First Floor . . . 1720 sq. ft.
Second Floor . . . 590 sq. ft.

PLAN 2414

The exterior of this home combines the traditional narrow clapboard with board and batten siding on the garage. The large central chimney, well-proportioned shutters and paneled entrance door with coach lantern are additional Early American details. First floor plan incudes the efficient U-shaped kitchen and formal dining room. The living room in the rear has a fireplace, as does the cozy study. Two bedrooms and two baths complete the ground level plan. Upstairs, to be finished now or later, are two bedrooms and a bath. Mirror reverse plans are available if specified at no additional cost. Materials list is included.

Designer: William M. Thompson, AIA

Creative styling for a two-story home

TO ORDER
BUILDING BLUEPRINTS
USE ORDER FORM
ON PAGE 111

PLAN 2327

A modest Colonial, this home features imaginative use of material and original design. For instance, the family room is highlighted by a soaring cathedral ceiling dominated by a large brick fireplace. To the right of the foyer is a formal dining room and, to the left, the living room. The kitchen-dinette area is partially open to the family room. The second floor provides two options: a three bedroom, dual entry bath plan, or a four bedroom, two full bath layout. Mirror reverse plans are available for $10 extra. Complete materials list is included.

Designer: Samuel Paul, AIA

First Floor . . . 1107 sq. ft.
Second Floor . . . 674 sq. ft.

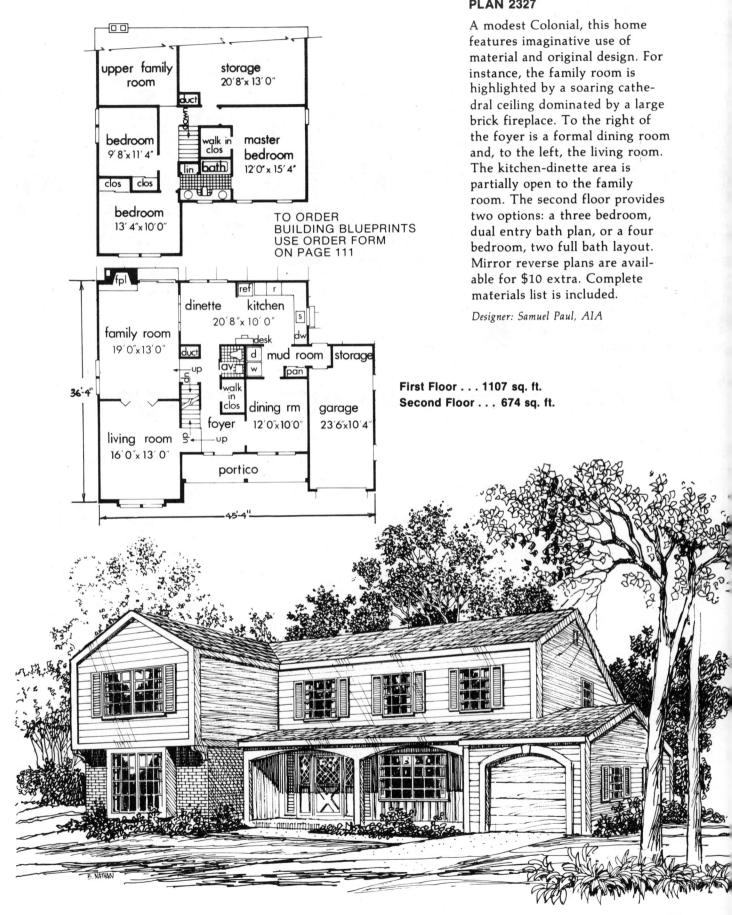

upper family room

storage
20'8" x 13'0"

duct
down

bedroom
9'8" x 11'4"

walk in clos

master bedroom
12'0" x 15'4"

clos clos

lin bath

bedroom
13'4" x 10'0"

fpl

ref r

dinette kitchen
20'8" x 10'0"

s

family room
19'0" x 13'0"

desk

dw

duct

d mud room storage

up

av

w

pan

walk in clos

dining rm
12'0" x 10'0"

garage
23'6" x 10'4"

36'-4"

living room
16'0" x 13'0"

up

foyer

up

portico

45'-4"

B. NATHAN

Good zoning and ample storage

PLAN 2030

This one and one-half story Early American home features a stone and clapboard exterior with high pitched roof line, central fireplace and other traditional details. The large living room with its bow window has log storage beside the fireplace. Efficient kitchen layout has breakfast area. The first floor plan contains two bedrooms and two baths. Two additional bedrooms and a bath complete the second floor. Mirror reverse plans are available if specified, and a materials list is included.

Designer: Master Plan Service

First Floor . . . 1505 sq. ft.
Second Floor . . .595 sq. ft.

Gambrel Colonial
with optional bedroom plan

PLAN 2247

This particularly pleasing exterior and well thought-out interior plan with optional three or four bedroom layout, provides a lot of comfort in only 1858 square feet of living space. The first floor offers a good-sized living room, formal dining room, L-shaped kitchen, handy utility room and a family room complete with fireplace, log storage area and access through the sliding glass doors to the rear patio. The second floor with two baths has a three or four bedroom option. Full materials list is included, and for an additional $30 full reverse plans are available for this Colonial.

Designer: National Plan Service

First Floor . . . 1046 sq. ft.
Second Floor . . . 812 sq. ft.

TO ORDER
BUILDING BLUEPRINTS
USE ORDER FORM
ON PAGE 111

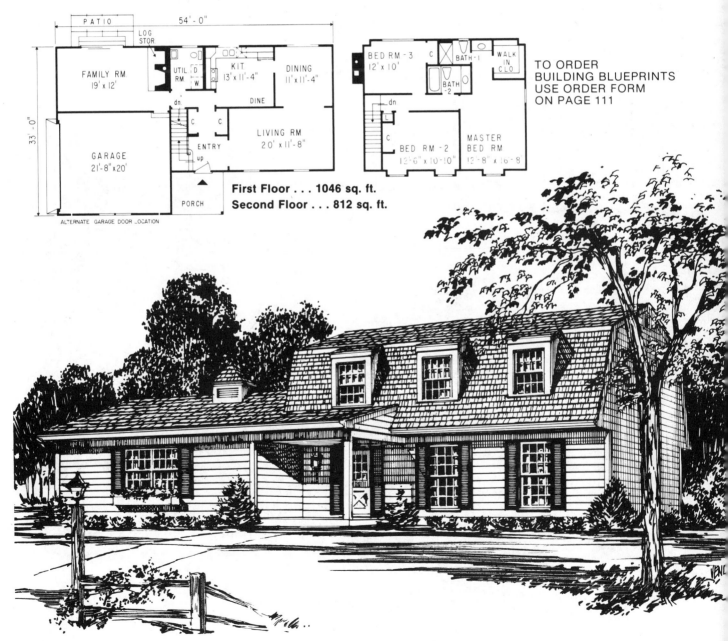

Exciting double chimney exterior

PLAN 2415

The exterior of this home has large brick chimneys at either side of the main structure, an architectural set back, and traditional clapboard combined with vertical wood siding to establish its Early American look. The shuttered windows and handsome panel entrance door with fluted columns and broken pediment detailing, complete the picture. Generous first floor rooms include the family room with fireplace, laundry, kitchen, snack area and formal dining room along the rear. The sunken living room has its own brick fireplace. Two baths and four bedrooms constitute the upstairs. Mirror reverse plans available if specified.

Designer: William M. Thompson, AIA

Second Floor . . . 1352 sq. ft.

BEDROOM 13'2 x 14'6
BATH
BATH
WALK-IN CLOSET
DN
BEDROOM 13'8 x 19'
BEDROOM 15'6 x 12'2
BEDROOM 13'2 x 11'4

First Floor . . . 1324 sq. ft.

DECK (OPTIONAL)
DINING ROOM 15'6 x 11'6
SNACK SPACE 7'6 x 11'2
KITCHEN 10'2 x 11'2
LAUNDRY MUD RM.
TWO CAR GARAGE 21'
LIVING ROOM 15'6 x 17'10
DN
UP
FAMILY ROOM 13'8 x 19'
ENTRANCE HALL
BAR
LAV.

36'-4"
68'-0"

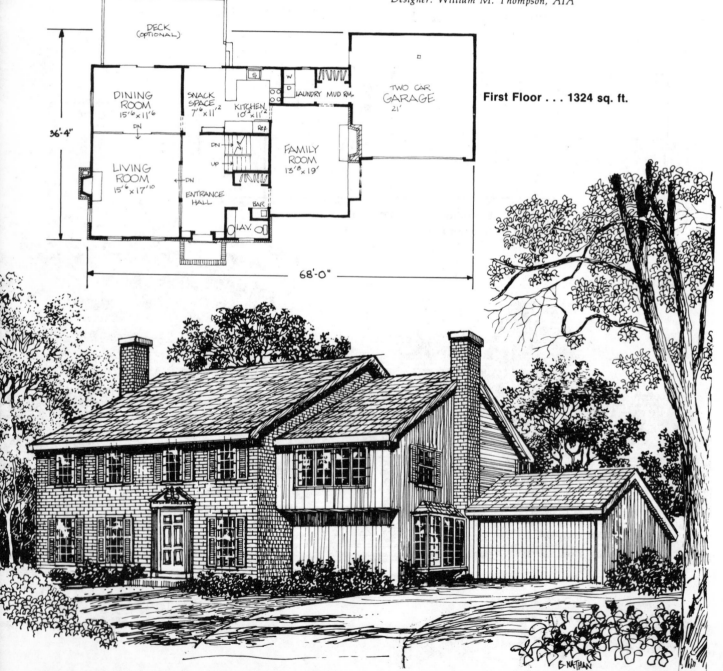

B. NATHAN

Charming two-bedroom Colonial

PLAN 5913

For young newlyweds or a retired couple, this plan is clean and compact. The one-story main structure is almost square in shape adding to the economy of construction. A third bedroom can be added in the rear later without loss of closet space. The large kitchen flows into the family-dining room with its comfortable fireplace. To the right of the entrance hall is the living room with fireplace. Two bedrooms and a full bath are at the rear of the home. Mirror reverse plans are available if specified at no additional cost. A materials list is included.

Designer: Evan Pollitt, Architect

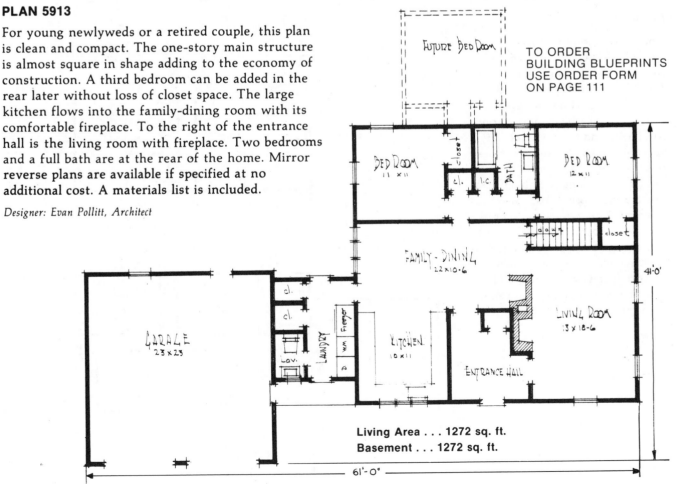

TO ORDER
BUILDING BLUEPRINTS
USE ORDER FORM
ON PAGE 111

Living Area . . . 1272 sq. ft.
Basement . . . 1272 sq. ft.

Careful planning assures privacy

PLAN 2039

The large family fortunate enough to own this warm and comfortable Colonial home will find the plan offers adequate space for everyone and everything. Five big bedrooms, three full baths and extensive closet space is zoned throughout the first and second floors. By locating all major plumbing in one compact area, costs are reduced. The generous covered breezeway between the house and garage provides a handy bad weather play area for children. Materials list is included, and mirror reverse plans are available if specified at no extra cost.

Designer: Master Plan Service

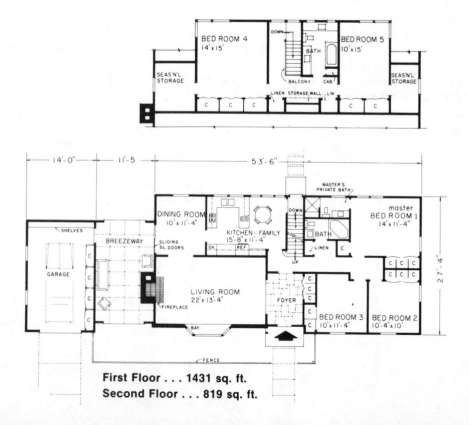

First Floor . . . 1431 sq. ft.
Second Floor . . . 819 sq. ft.

Southern Colonial for contemporary living

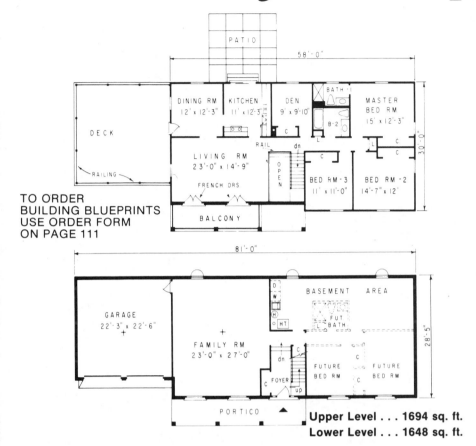

TO ORDER
BUILDING BLUEPRINTS
USE ORDER FORM
ON PAGE 111

Upper Level . . . 1694 sq. ft.
Lower Level . . . 1648 sq. ft.

PLAN 2248

Style, charm and space are offered in this large traditional home easily adaptable to a difficult building site. From the entrance foyer in the lower level, stairs lead upward to a large living room with double french doors opening onto the front balcony. Three bedrooms, two baths, a private den, kitchen and formal dining room with door to the large deck over the garage complete the upper portion. Lower level contains family room and space for future two bedrooms and a bath. Materials list included; full reverse plans are available for $30 extra.

Designer: National Plan Service

TO ORDER
BUILDING BLUEPRINTS
USE ORDER FORM
ON PAGE 111

Pleasing proportions with bedroom option

PLAN 4320

The simple, clean lines of the exterior of this home are subtly accented by a gently arched portico. The foyer divides the living area on the right from the sleeping wing on the left with the master bedroom and bath, plus two additional bedrooms and a bath. Optional two bedroom first floor plan is available. The second floor contains two bedrooms and a bath. Kitchen and breakfast area adjoin family room with fireplace and sliding door to rear sun deck. Mirror reverse plans are available if specified at no additional cost. Complete materials list is available for $10.

Designer: W. D. Farmer

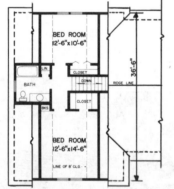

First Floor . . . 1821 sq. ft.
Second Floor . . . 542 sq. ft.
Basement . . . 1821 sq. ft.

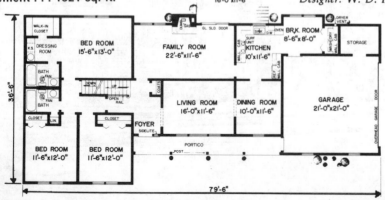

TO ORDER
BUILDING BLUEPRINTS
USE ORDER FORM
ON PAGE 111

Exciting home planning ideas.

Ideas for every facet of home planning, home plans in every architectural style that you can buy and build, as well as a complete guide to your home product needs and a practical solution to the mysteries of solar energy systems are yours direct from the Bantam/Hudson Planning Center.
See order form below.

Bantam/Hudson Plans Books

An outstanding collection of home plans to buy, in every architectural style. Designs for every section of the country at a price you can afford. Also Home Improvement Projects. Each $2.95.

    100 Custom Homes Plans 112 pages
    Colonial Home Plans 112 pages
    Contemporary Home Plans 112 pages
    Small Home Plans 112 pages
    Leisure Home Plans 112 pages
    Home Improvement Project Ideas
                          80 pages

Complete Home Catalog

The first comprehensive source book of where-to-get-it information. A practical guide to building products for homeowner or professional. Includes the Automatic Secretary to get you additional information on any subject covered. 350 plus pages, $7.95 + $1.45 postage and handling.

Bantam/Hudson Idea Books

A picture-packed series of elegant home planning ideas for your new home, your vacation home or that long-planned remodeling project designed to make your home a better place to live. Each $4.95.

    Kitchen Ideas 112 pages
    Bathroom Ideas 112 pages
    Decks and Patios 112 pages
    Fireplace Ideas 112 pages
    Remodeling Ideas 128 pages
    Bonus Rooms 128 pages
    Bedroom Ideas 128 pages
    Vacation Homes 128 pages

A Practical Guide to Solar Homes

All the basic information you need if you are thinking solar. Includes thirty solar and energy-conserving home plans to buy and a comprehensive listing of products on the market. 144 pages, $6.95.

Manufacturers' Index

Appliances

Amana Refrigeration, Inc.
Amana, IA 52204

American Gas Assn.
1515 Wilson Blvd.
Arlington, VA 22209

Caloric Corp.
18444 West 10 Mile Rd.
Topton, PA 19562

Distinctive Appliances, Inc.
8826 Lankershim Blvd.
Sun Valley, CA 91352

Frigidaire Div.,
General Motors Corp.
300 Taylor St.
Dayton, OH 45442

General Electric Co.
2100 Gardiner Ln.
Louisville, KY 40205

Hardwick Stove Co.
240 Edward St.
Cleveland, TN 37311

Hotpoint Div., GE Co.
2100 Gardiner Ln.
Louisville, KY 40205

In-Sink-Erator Div.,
Emerson Electric Co.
4700 21st St.
Racine, WI 53406

Jenn-Air Corp.
3035 N. Shadeland Ave.
Indianapolis, IN 46226

Magic Chef, Inc.
Box 717
Cleveland, TN 37311

Modern Maid, Div.
McGraw-Edison Co.
Box 1111
Chattanooga, TN 37401

Monarch Range Co.
715 North Spring St.
Beaver Dam, WI 53916

Norris Industries, Thermador/Waste King Div.
5119 District Blvd.
Los Angeles, CA 90022

Ronson Corp.
One Ronson Rd.
Woodbridge, NJ 07095

Tappan Appliance Corp.
Tappan Park
Mansfield, OH 44901

Cabinets

Connor Forest Inds.
Box 847
Wausau, WI 54401

Coppes, Inc.
455 E. Market St.
Nappanee, IN 46550

Excel Wood Products Co.
Box 819
Lakewood, NJ 08701

International Paper Co.,
Cabinet Div.
Box 8411
Portland, OR 97207

IXL, Div. Westinghouse
Electric Corp.
R. R. 1
Elizabeth City, NC 27909

Merillat Industries, Inc.
2075 W. Beecher Rd.
Adrian, MI 49221

Mutschler Bros. Co.
South Madison St.
Nappanee, IN 46550

Quaker Maid Kitchens,
Div. Tappan Co.
Rt. 61
Leesport, PA 19533

Riviera Products
1960 Seneca Rd.
St. Paul, MN 55122

H. J. Scheirich Co.
Box 21037
Louisville, KY 40221

St. Charles Mfg. Co.
551 Tyler Rd.
St. Charles, IL 60174

Triangle Pacific Cabinet Corp.
4255 LBJ Freeway
Dallas, TX 75234

United Cabinet Corp.
Box 420
Jasper, IN 47546

Exterior Building Materials

Bird & Son
Washington St.
East Walpole, MA 02032

Caradco Div., Scovill Mfg. Co.
1098 Jackson St.
Dubuque, IA 52001

Certain-teed Products Corp.
Box 860
Valley Forge, PA 19482

Johns-Manville Sales Co.
Greenwood Plaza
Denver, CO 80217

E. A. Nord Co.
Box 1187
Everett, WA 98206

Shakertown Corp.
Box 400
Winlock, WA 98596

Fireplaces

Atlanta Stove Works
Box 5254
Atlanta, GA 30307

Dyna Corp.
2540 Industry Way
Lynwood, CA 90262

Heatilator Div.,
Vega Industries
W. Saunders St.
Mt. Pleasant, IA 52641

The Majestic Co.
245 Erie St.
Huntington, IN 46750

Malm Fireplaces, Inc.
368 Yolanda Ave.
Santa Rosa, CA 95404

Portland Stove Foundry
57 Kennebec St.
Portland, ME 04104

Portland Willamette Co.
6800 N.E. 59th Pl.
Portland, OR 97218

Preway, Inc.
1430 2nd St., N.
Wisconsin Rapids, WI 54494

Superior Fireplace Co.
4325 Artesia Ave.
Fullterton, CA 92633

Washington Stove Works
Box 687
Everett, WA 98201

Western Fireplaces/
A. R. Wood Mfg. Co.
Box 218
Luverne, MN 56156

Floorcoverings

American Olean Tile Co.
1000 Cannon Ave.
Lansdale, PA 19446

Armstrong Cork Co.
Lancaster, PA 17604

Azrock Floor Products
Box 531
San Antonio, TX 78292

Bangkok Industries
1900 S. 20th St.
Philadelphia, PA 19145

Bissell, Inc.
Box 1888
Grand Rapids, MI 49501

E. L. Bruce Co., Inc.
Box 16902
Memphis, TN 38116

Congoleum Corp.
195 Belgrove Dr.
Kearny, NJ 07032

Ege Rya, Inc.
919 Third Ave.
New York, NY 10022

GAF Corp.
140 W. 51st St.
New York, NY 10020

Kentile Floors, Inc.
58 2nd Ave.
Brooklyn, NY 11215

Memphis Hardwood Flooring
1551 Thomas St.
Memphis, TN 38107

National Floor
Products, Inc.
P. O. Box 354
Florence, AL 35630

Peace Flooring Co.
Box 87
Magnolia, AK 71753

Sturbridge Yankee Workshop
573 Brimfield Turnpike
Sturbridge, MA 01566

Tile Council of America
P. O. Box 503
Mahwah, NJ 07430

U. S. Ceramic Tile Co.
1375 Raff Rd., S. W.
Canton, OH 44710

Wood Mosaic
Box 21159
Louisville, KY 40221

Furniture

American Drew, Inc.
Box 489
No. Wilkesboro, NC 28659

Baker Furniture Co.
474 Merchandise Mart
Chicago, IL 60654

The Bartley Collection, Ltd.
747 Oakwood Ave.
Lake Forest, IL 60045

Bassett Furniture Industries
Bassett, VA 24055

Broyhill Furniture
Box 700
Lenoir, NC 28633

Cochrane Furniture
P. O. Box 220
Lincolnton, NC 28092

Craft House, Colonial
Williamsburg Foundation
Williamsburg, VA 23185

DeSoto Furniture
Box 492
Jackson, MS 39205

Drexel-Heritage Furniture
16 Hufman Rd.
Drexel, NC 28619

Ethan Allen, Inc.
Allen Dr.
Danbury, CT 06810

Founders Furniture
P. O. Box 339
Thomasville, NC 27360

Guild of Shaker Crafts
401 Savidge St.
Spring Lake, MI 49456

Hagerty Co.
38 Parker Ave.
Cohasset, MA 02025

Harden Furniture Co.
McConnellsville, NY 13401

Henredon Furniture
Industries, Inc.
Morganton, NC 28655

Heywood-Wakefield Co.
206 Central
Gardner, MA 01440

Hickory Furniture Co.
Hickory, NC 28601

The Hitchcock Chair Co.
Riverton, CT 06065

Howard Family Room
Furnishings
Box 732
Starksville, MS 39759

Hooker Furniture Corp.
P. O. Box 4708
Martinsville, VA 24112

Kimball International
1549 Royal St.
Jasper, IN 47546

Kindel Furniture Co.
100 Garden S. E.
Grand Rapids, MI 49502

Kittinger Co.
1893 Elmwood Ave.
Buffalo, NY 14207

Kroehler Mfg. Co.
222 E. 5th St.
Naperville, IL 60540

MaLeck Woodcraft
Wingate, NC 28174

Thos. Moser Cabinet Maker
26 Cobb's Bridge Rd.
New Gloucester, ME 04260

Pennsylvania House, Div.
General Interiors Corp.
North 10th St.
Lewisburg, PA 17837

Peters-Revington
100 N. Washington St.
Delphi, IN 46923

Pulaski Furniture Corp.
P. O. Box 1371
Pulaski, VA 24301

Shaker Workshops, Inc.
P. O. Box 710
Concord, MA 01742

Simmons Co.
2 Park Ave.
New York, NY 10016

Stanley Furniture Co.
Stanleytown, VA 24168

Sturbridge Yankee Workshop
Sturbridge, MA 01566

Tell City Chair Co.
Tell City, IN 47586

Thomasville Furniture
Inds., Inc.
P. O. Box 339
Thomasville, NC 27360

Paints & Stains

Samuel Cabot, Inc.
One Union St.
Boston, MA 02108

Cohasset Colonials
Cohasset, MA 02025

Celanese Corp. of America
1211 Ave. of Americas
New York, NY 10036

Champion Building Products
One Landmark Square
Stamford, CT 06921

Devoe Paint Co.
Box 1863
Louisville, KY 40201

Glidden-Durkee, Div. SCM
900 Union Comm. Bldg.
Cleveland, OH 44115

Martin Senour Paints
2500 S. Senour Ave.
Chicago, IL 60608

Benjamin Moore & Co.
51 Chestnut Ridge Rd.
Montvale, NJ 07645

Olympic Stain, Div.
Comerco, Inc.
1148 N. W. Leary Way
Seattle, WA 98107

Pittsburg Paints, PPG
Industries, Inc.
One Gateway Center
Pittsburgh, PA 15222

The Sherwin Williams Co.
101 Prospect Ave., N. W.
Cleveland, OH 44101

Wallcoverings

Brunschwig & Fils, Inc.
410 E. 62nd St.
New York, NY 10021

Craft House, Colonial
Williamsburg Foundation
Williamsburg, VA 23185

Jack Denst Designs
7355 South Exchange Ave.
Chicago, IL 60649

Ethan Allen, Inc.
Allen Dr.
Danbury, CT 06810

Georgia-Pacific Corp.
900 S. W. 5th Ave.
Portland, OR 97204

Masonite Corp.
29 N. Wacker Dr.
Chicago, IL 60606

Reed Wallcoverings
550 Pharr Rd.
Atlanta, GA 30305

Thomas Strahan Co.
150 Heard St.
Chelsea, MA 02150

Albert Van Luit & Co.
4000 Chevy Chase Dr.
Los Angeles, CA 90039

Wallcovering Industry Bureau
1099 Wall St., West
Lyndhurst, NJ 07071

How To Order Your Home Plans

- Enter plan number and number of sets wanted on order form as indicated.
- Mirror Reverse plans have all lettering and dimensions reading backwards—you will need at least two sets; one regular and one in mirror reverse.
- Materials lists and reverse plans are available only when noted in plans copy.
- Specify on order form if you want reverse plans or materials lists.
- Quality lists do not list quantities needed.

- If you plan to build, we suggest a minimum of 4–6 sets for your lender, builder, subcontractors, local building departments, etc.
- PLANS HOTLINE — You may speed your plans order by dialing TOLL FREE 800-227-8393. (California residents phone direct 415-941-6700.) For Master Charge or VISA/BankAmericard cardholders only. (Sorry, no C.O.D.'s.)

Plan Prices

1 set $75; 4 sets $105; 8 sets $148; each additional set $12.

Plan	Page	Plan	Page	Plan	Page	Plan	Page	Plan	Page	Plan	Page
2030	100	2246	89	2411	56	3321	74	4207	34	5904	10
2033	11	2247	101	2412	63	3323	20	4208	42	5905	17
2034	19	2248	105	2413	90	3324	40	4209	73	5906	21
2035	32	2318	22	2414	98	3325	55	4210	94	5907	38
2036	35	2322	14	2415	102	3326	62	4212	18	5908	45
2037	46	2324	33	2710	59	3327	95	4311	24	5909	60
2039	104	2325	39	2718	58	3411	13	4315	16	5910	76
2241	23	2326	44	2720	15	3412	93	4316	26	5911	88
2242	61	2327	99	2721	43	3519	36	4317	41	5912	96
2243	75	2402	25	2723	72	3864	79	4318	47	5913	103
2244	77	2409	27	2724	92	4204	12	4319	91		
2245	78	2410	37	2725	97	4206	57	4320	106		

Mail to: **HOME PLANS**
Hudson Home Publications
289 S. San Antonio Rd.
Los Altos, Calif. 94022

Order Form

Please send me _____ sets of

blueprints for Plan No. _____ Cost: $ _____

Send Complete Home Catalog, too ($7.95) .... $ _____

Postage and Handling .... $ __2.50__

Allow 10 working days for delivery

California Residents add 6% Sales Tax .... $ _____

TOTAL $ _____

I hereby authorize Hudson Publishing Company to execute a sales slip on my behalf against my ☐ Master Charge ☐ VISA/BankAmericard

in the amount of $ _____ Card Exp. Date _____

Your Signature _____

Name (print) _____

Address _____

City _____

State _____ Zip _____

Make check or Money Order Payable to Hudson Home Publications/RCL
(Sorry, no C.O.D.'s)

Mail to: **HOME PLANS**
Hudson Home Publications
289 S. San Antonio Rd.
Los Altos, Calif. 94022

Order Form

Please send me _____ sets of

blueprints for Plan No. _____ Cost: $ _____

Send Complete Home Catalog, too ($7.95) ...... $ _____

Postage and Handling .... $ __2.50__

Allow 10 working days for delivery

California Residents add 6% Sales Tax .... $ _____

TOTAL $ _____

I hereby authorize Hudson Publishing Company to execute a sales slip on my behalf against my ☐ Master Charge ☐ VISA/BankAmericard

in the amount of $ _____ Card Exp. Date _____

Your Signature _____

Name (print) _____

Address _____

City _____

State _____ Zip _____

Make check or Money Order Payable to Hudson Home Publications/RCL
(Sorry, no C.O.D.'s)